*A Journal Retreat*

# Christ Encounters

*Gloria Hutchinson*

## DATE DUE

| | | | |
|---|---|---|---|
| | | | |
| | | | |
| | | | |
| | | | |
| | | | |
| | | | |
| | | | |
| | | | |
| | | | |
| | | | |
| | | | |
| | | | |
| | | | |
| | | | |
| | | | |
| | | | |
| | | | |
| | | | Printed in USA |

# Christ
## Encounters

*A Journal Retreat*

# Christ Encounters

*Gloria Hutchinson*

**AVE MARIA PRESS**
NOTRE DAME, INDIANA 46556

Excerpts from the NEW JERUSALEM BIBLE, copyright © 1985 by
Darton, Longman & Todd, Ltd. and Doubleday and Company, Inc.
Reprinted by permission of the publisher.

Library of Congress Catalog Card Number: 88-70575
International Standard Book Number: 0-87793-378-2
Cover Design: Katherine A. Coleman
Printed and bound in the United States of America.

*For Carole Jean and all who will encounter Christ in these pages*

*"The entire meaning and content of the Bible is to be found, say the Apostles, not in the message about Christ but in an encounter with Christ."*

Thomas Merton
Opening the Bible

# Contents

## Part One: Seeking Guidance

## Part Two: Seeking Growth

## Part Three: Seeking Glory

# Preface

---

*Christ Encounters* is a 30-day at-home retreat for anyone who wants to come apart with the Rabbi from Nazareth and risk the consequences.

The journal format encourages retreatants to respond in writing day by day to the gospel stories and their related reflections. The journal questions pin down, in black and white, how the reader feels he or she is doing in specific areas of spiritual growth. They provide grist for the closing ''Retreat Decisions'' about conversion and/or renewed commitment.

Each day's meditation—which may be done in 15 minutes but done better in 30—focuses on a question Jesus raised with his followers. It is based on the conviction that the Lord aims those same inquiries at his contemporary disciples and asks, ''So, what do you think?''

Karl Barth once observed, ''When you begin to question the Bible, you find that the Bible is also questioning you.'' If I go to the Good Book, wondering who this Jesus really is, the Book comes back at me with ''Who do you say he is?'' or, more impertinently, ''Who wants to know?''

When Job, browbeaten by misfortune and propped up against a dung heap, tries to question God about the cause and the justification for his suffering (''Why do you choose me as your target? . . . Is it right for you to attack me? . . . Why did you bring me out of the womb?''), what answer does he get?

From the heart of the tempest, Yahweh God responds:

Who is this, obscuring my intentions with his ignorant words?
Brace yourself like a fighter;
I am going to ask the questions, and you are to inform me!
(Job 38: 2-3).

God turns the tables on Job. Answers, like signs, are not given on demand.

Jesus lures his disciples into dialogue, attempting to draw the truth out of them like a woman determined to hoist water from a deep well: ''What gain, then, is it for anyone to win the whole world and forfeit his life?''

The Bible challenges us with a question for every answer it divulges. If we hold up our end of the relationship, we discover not only who God is but who, in reality, we are. That's what makes the questions of Jesus so vital to us. They are a matter of life or death. For if I do not know who God sees in me, do I truly have life?

# Prayer Before Each Day's Encounter

Jesus, just and loving
Inquisitor of hearts,
I train my attention
entirely on You.
Open my eyes
to see You,
my ears
to hear You,
my heart,
to encounter You.
Question me
and I will inform You.
Amen.

*Part One*
*Seeking Guidance*

Finding a good spiritual director is no easy task. Maybe that's why I've always envied the Desert Fathers and Mothers. These early Christian hermits, who fled the pagan cities in search of salvation, were masters of the practical word of advice. And there were plenty of them to go around. Whenever a young brother or sister needed guidance, there always seemed to be a wise abba or amman at hand to oblige.

Here, for example, is a typical dialogue:

Brother: Abba, what is humility?
Elder:   To do good to those who do evil to you.
Brother: Supposing a person can't go that far. What should he do?
Elder:   Let him get away from them and keep his mouth shut.
         (From *The Wisdom of the Desert*, Thomas Merton, New York: New Directions, 1970, pp. 53-54.)

This straight-from-the-hip style of question and answer is found repeatedly in the gospel accounts of how Jesus guided those who aspired to discipleship. They come to him saying, in one way or another, "What should we do?" or "How should we live?" and he responds with a cryptic comment ("It is not the healthy who need the doctor, but the sick."), a provocative little story ("Listen, a sower went out to sow. . ."), or a plain-spoken inquiry of his own ("Why do you ask me about what is good?").

If we are as sincere as the first-century disciples and the fourth-century hermits about seeking spiritual guidance, we can come apart with Christ, encounter him in dialogue, take his questions—and our own answers—to heart.

Finding a good spiritual director is no easy task. But the gospel is a promising place to start.

# *Day 1*   *What do you want?* (Jn 1:38)

*Scripture context: Jn 1:35-40*

---

"I have often walked down this street before," sings the beguiled suitor, his tenor voice swelling precipitously. "But the pavement always stayed beneath my feet before." The scene from *My Fair Lady* taps into that familiar vein of rapture that overflows when we approach the place where a loved one resides. Eliza Doolittle's pursuer is inflated with cloud-castle images of encountering her at any second. He is overpowered by the sense that her presence pervades the entire neighborhood like a two-liter atomizer of French perfume.

Love's ability to transform an Archie Bunker flat into an Astaire-Rogers ballroom set is a romantic fact of life. Yet the range of love's transmuting is hardly bound by boy-meets-girl. When I approach a close friend's house after long separation, my eyes discern a place of far greater promise than the yellow clapboards and black shutters suggest to casual passers-by. When I return to a church or a retreat house where I was once kindled by some seraphic liturgical high, memory boosts my blood pressure at first glimpse of the bell tower.

Happily, we never outgrow the desire to find and inhabit the place where our true love lives. Whether we search in a lover's darkened hiding place or a friend's well-lit window, in the unqualified embrace of a mother or of a community, our quarry remains the same. We know love by many names, one of which is home.

When John the Baptist pointed at Jesus and announced, "Look! There is the Lamb of God!" two of his disciples sat up and took notice. They knew the prophet was onto something. An ordinary morning had been blown wide open by anticipation.

The one John had testified to on the previous day looked as common as the shepherds who slept with their flocks in the Galilean hills. But there was a compelling quality to the way he walked (as though he were on his way to the Temple at Passover) and to the way he had glanced at them as he passed (like one who knew secrets about them they had not yet suspected themselves).

To say they made a decision to follow him would be to overstate the case. They were drawn—overpowered—yanked out of their usual selves. Andrew and the other disciple fell in behind Jesus the Nazarene, sticking to his heels like hot-blooded youths after an idolized rebel leader. John, whom they revered, was temporarily nullified. They had no idea where they were going. Nor did they ask. Jesus, pleased, led them a ways without comment.

Would they persist in tagging along? Or would they soon think better of their impulsive behavior? Jesus gave them time to change their minds. Then he turned and said, "What do you want?"

Did his voice convey only curiosity? Or did he feign a note of impatience to test their resolve? If so, the question may have sounded more like "So what are you two up to?" or "What are you after, anyway?"

Considering his situation (an unknown and unlikely messiah about to enlist his first followers) Jesus may have had a hard time not laughing out loud at the rash fidelity of Andrew and his companion. Would all his disciples come so readily? He had made no speeches, offered no promises. Yet there the two of them were, apparently wanting nothing more than to keep him company and to see where he lived. But before he could invite them into his lodging, Jesus had to elicit a response.

"What do you want?"

"Rabbi," they said, honoring him with the title, "where do you live?"

That's all they asked. And with those few words of trust, a relationship was born. They didn't inquire about what he might do for them. They didn't ask to see his teaching credentials. They simply wanted to go home with him—sensing even then that home was where he was.

Although they loved the Baptist, they had readily left him for this man whom John had identified as the Chosen One. They didn't hang back, waiting for wiser heads than theirs to decide what should be done. They saw him pass by and they followed him.

"So they went and saw where he lived and stayed with him that day." However humble the house may have been, the disciples would ever after remember it as a place of light and beauty. They hung on Jesus' words like willing fish on a line. He took delight in their attention, laying out his best truths for them to taste. They felt they had always known him. Or perhaps that they had always wanted to know one like him, so passionate in faith, so forthright in friendship. Darkness came as a rude intrusion. They didn't want to leave him.

Years later as they recalled that first day when his appearance had so transported them, Andrew and his companion laughed and sang of that overpowering feeling that had carried them out of themselves.

*Lord, make us foolish enough to set out at your heels without first requiring a detailed itinerary.*

*Consider:*

Today Jesus asks you, "What do you want?" Relax in his presence and ponder what your response might be in light of the retreat you are undertaking. (Write your response so that it does not disappear in the never-never land of forgetfulness.)

*Act:*

What might you do today (or soon) to experience Jesus himself as the answer to this question?

# Day 2   *(Woman), what do you want from me?*
*(Jn 2:4)*

*Scripture context: Jn 2:1-11*

---

When a South Korean sea captain encountered a small boat overloaded with Vietnamese refugees in the South China Sea, he knew that, as a practical matter, it was no concern of his. His cargo was expected in Bangkok at a prearranged time. Other ships would soon come along and someone would pick up these strays.

However, the persistent cries and waves of the refugees eventually won Captain Go Jong-Ryeong over. He could not steel his heart against the pleading of those who were so obviously depending on him to do something. Although it wasn't the place or the time he would have chosen, Go Jong-Ryeong stopped to take aboard the 63 stranded refugees. He said he did it as a sign of his respect for life.

There may be a slightly off-center parallel between this story and that of the wedding at Cana. Mary, speaking for the newlyweds who are stranded in the middle of their reception without a shred of hope to cling to, says to Jesus, "They have no more wine."

A Jewish wedding feast at which the wine barrels had run dry would be far more calamitous than an Irish wake with nary a drop of 100-proof Irish whiskey. For the Israelites, wine was the elixir of their espousal to Yahweh. Out of respect for the joyful covenant life that was theirs alone, they could not properly celebrate a marital union without it. None of this is lost on Mary.

She doesn't say what she expects Jesus to do. But she is unmistakably depending on him to save the bridal couple from certain disaster. There is no practical reason why Jesus should be burdened with this responsibility. He could, like Captain Jong-Ryeong, safely say that those in distress were not his problem.

So, blunt as can be, he says, "Woman, how does this concern of yours involve me? My hour has not yet come." His mother's expectations do not agree with his own self-understanding. This is not the place or the time to call up the creative power his Father has invested in him. He addresses Mary as "Woman" (rather like our "Madam") to let her know that her maternal privileges are not to be invoked here.

Does Mary say, "Alright, son. I'm sorry I asked "? Strong-minded mother that she must have been, she says nothing. What her black eyes communicated to this full-grown man who would always be her boy we can only guess. Despite his refusal, Mary trusts that Jesus will act. Believing in the rightness of her request, she doesn't take no for an answer.

Unable to steel his heart against her—or the entire wedding party for whom she is the advocate—Jesus sighs, stands up and asks that six stone jars be filled with water. When the head waiter samples the "water" from one of the jars, he purses his lips reflectively and then breaks into a beatific smile. The wily groom, it seems, has turned the tables by saving the superior wine for the party's denouement. What a coup! The reputation of the newlyweds is now guaranteed.

Contemporary scripture scholars, trying to wean us away from interpreting this story as a proof of Mary's intercessory power, point out that she is really depicted as a person of imperfect faith and limited understanding of who Jesus is at this early stage of his ministry. In all her good intentions and implicit trust, she turns to Jesus. He says, "Why do you ask this of me?" It sounds like "Forget it. It's none of my business. If you really knew me, you wouldn't ask."

Yet, what happens? Mary says to the waiter, "Do whatever he tells you." And Jesus, won over by the simplicity of her persistent faith in him, complies. One day Mary will stand by him on Calvary like the mature disciple she has become. However, Jesus doesn't require a fully informed faith as a prerequisite from those who seek his help. His no becomes yes in the face of trusting reliance.

*Lord, when we are stranded on trouble's edge, remind us of the wine that was your vibrant yes to life.*

*Consider:*

Like Mary at Cana, we still have a lot to learn about who Jesus is and what it means to be faithful disciples. Reflect on whether there is one gift, quality or virtue which, by its comparative absence, threatens your spiritual progress. Compose your own brief dialogue with Jesus on this topic. Imagine that his initial response sounds like ''Woman (or Sir), what do you want from me?'' What might your answer be?

*Act:*

What will you say or do to demonstrate your faith in the face of a seemingly negative response from the Lord?

*Day 3*     *You know me and you know where I come from?*(Jn 7:28, RSV)

*Scripture context: Jn 7:14-31*

---

Thomas Merton in *The Wisdom of the Desert* relates an ancient story about a group of monks who went out from their monastery to visit the hermits who lived in the Egyptian desert. These fifth-century hermits were renowned for their asceticism and solitary lifestyle. They were the major league champs when it came to self-abnegation. When the monks (the minor leaguers) arrived at the first hermitage, their host received them gladly and set out all the food he had for the evening meal.

That night, when the visitors thought the hermit was asleep, they gossiped about how much food he had. Surely these solitaries did not deserve their reputation as spiritual athletes who had far outdistanced their cenobitic brothers.

The next morning before the visitors departed for the next hermitage, their host gave them a message, ''Greet my brother for me and tell him not to water the vegetables.'' The second hermit understood the coded message immediately. He invited the guests to join him in weaving baskets all day long—with no breaks for meals. At night he added several psalms to the prayers before supper. Then he served dry bread and salt.

After clutching their growling stomachs all night, the monks tried to make a quick escape in the morning. But the hermit insisted that charity required him to offer them hospitality for several days. Once it was dark again, the disgruntled visitors slunk off to the comfort of their monastery. Their propensity for judging by appearances had left them hungry—and humbled.

A certain carpenter's son from Nazareth evoked the same kind of response from many of his fellow Jews who judged him an unworthy messiah. Despite the indisputable charism and authority of his preaching, they remained impervious to his instruction. Because Jesus lacked the proper educational, social and religious credentials, he was persona non grata with the skeptics. For the aristocratic Sadducees, he was too common; for the self-righteous Pharisees, too lenient. He enjoyed eating and drinking too much and said too little about fasting. Some labeled him ''a glutton and a drunkard.''

By all appearances, Jesus was as ordinary as any other Nazarene laborer. His hands still bore the trademark callouses of a carpenter. His weathered face gave evidence that he had not spent his days theologizing in the synagogue. Thus, many Jews could not accept him as the Son of God. They knew where he was from, who his parents were and how he had earned his living. What else did they need to know? For them, Jesus was a gifted preacher and a wonder worker. But he was also a deluded troublemaker. His critics had to wonder why he hadn't been taken into custody by the high priest.

Angered by their clucking and carping, Jesus cries out, "You know me and you know where I come from?" They stare, uncomprehending, wondering what he's up to. Will he deny his modest origins? His authority, he tells them, comes from God. And they know as little about God as they know about him. Seeking spiritual guidance, they yet prefer to go hungry rather than accept food from a messiah not made in their own image. He isn't good enough for them.

Some are determined to grab him and put him out of circulation. But, like the hometown crowd that tried to hurl him over a cliff after he'd identified himself in the synagogue, they cannot lay a hand on him. His hour has not yet come.

Others of his critics, jolted by Jesus' unexpected question, are now ready to admit they've been blind fools. "When the Christ appears," they ask, "will he do more signs than this man has done?" They, at least, have learned to look beyond their stunted preconceptions.

Isaiah says of the Savior, "Not by appearances shall he judge, nor by hearsay shall he decide" (Is 11:3). The monks who misjudged the hospitable hermit denied themselves an opportunity for enlightenment, just as the Jews who denied Jesus' authenticity were left to their own meager resources.

Both stories give us pause. Is it possible that we too have failed to recognize the Christ who did not fit our image of how the Savior should look and sound and act in today's world?

*Oh, Jesus, we hardly knew ye.*

*Consider:*

Are you inclined to judge potential spiritual directors or guides on the basis of appearance (not how they look but how well they fit your image of a Christian guru)? Why or why not?

For instance, if you are a woman, do you accept the possibility of another woman (religious or lay) directing your spiritual development?

If you are a religious or priest, are you open to the guidance wise and discerning lay persons may offer?

How will you interpret and respond to "You know me and you know where I come from?"

*Act:*

How will you avoid judging by appearances when it comes to seeing Christ in potential spiritual guides?

# Day 4 — Do you believe in the Son of man?
(Jn 9:35)

*Scripture context: Jn 9:1-41*

---

The scene from Act IV of *King Lear* leaves a sour taste in the mouth, a clot of impotent anger in the throat. The ancient monarch, driven mad by his daughters' heartless schemes and his own folly, encounters the Earl of Gloucester, who has been blinded by the order of his own pitiless son. Both men suffer the knowledge that they are despised by their offspring. Shakespeare, playing artfully on the theme of their willful blindness, then leads Lear and Gloucester into newfound insight.

The King observes to his sightless friend, "A man may see how this world goes with no eyes. Look with thine ears." In the past, he has seen and believed only what reinforced his pride and paternal vanity. By choosing to remain blind to the truth about his daughters Goneril and Regan, who deceived him with flattery and false affection, Lear has been undone. Now he says bitterly to Gloucester,

> Get thee glass eyes,
> And, like a scurvy politician, seem
> To see the things thou dost not.
> (Act IV, scene vi)

Transposed to a gospel context, those lines could aptly apply not to a scurvy politician but a supercilious Pharisee. For Jesus, the Pharisees personify a willful blindness to the "light of the world." Their glass eyes see images projected by their own censoriousness; they perceive faults where none exist.

In the story of the man born blind, Jesus gives sight to a beggar whom many can attest has been stone blind from the cradle. The man's impairment will allow "God's work to be shown forth in him." Jesus then urges his disciples to get on with God's work while they are still in daylight.

Despite the irrefutability of that light (with which Jesus has identified himself), the Pharisees refuse to believe in the miracle or the One who made it happen. Their pride and professional religious vanity allow them to view Jesus as a sinner who does not keep the sabbath according to their proscriptions. ("This man cannot be from God because he does not keep the sabbath!") To separate themselves further from the upstart messiah, they claim exclusive allegiance to Moses with whom God spoke on Sinai. With absolute surety, they protest the very possibility that God is the place where Jesus comes from.

When the Pharisees try to disprove the miracle, the contrast between their blindly self-righteous protestations and the lucid defense of the beggar is hilarious. Picture it as a slapstick routine with PeeWee Herman as the beggar and Don Rickles as the lead Pharisee.

Pharisee: We know that God spoke to Moses, but as for this man, we don't know where he comes from.

Beggar: That is just what is so amazing! *(He raises his eyebrows and lifts his hands imploringly to the heavens, seeking light on this contradiction.)* We know that God doesn't listen to sinners, but God listens to men who are devout and do his will. *(He stares bug-eyed at his interlocutors lest they miss the too obvious point.)* Ever since the world began it is unheard of for anyone to open the eyes of a man who was born blind; if this man were not from God, he wouldn't have been able to do anything. *(He sits emphatically, using his body as a gavel announcing "Case dismissed!")*

Pharisee: *(With a cold blast of pomposity)* Are you trying to teach us, and you a sinner through and through ever since you were born! *(Smack. Thwack. You impertinent layman!)*

When Jesus hears that his beggar friend has been thrown out on his ear, he seeks him out with the intention of offering him something far more valuable than eyesight. First comes the inevitable question, "Do you believe in the Son of man?"

Speaking with 20/20 vision, the man replies, "Sir, tell me who he is so that I may believe in him?" Jesus, welcoming this unarmed response, says, "You have seen him. He is speaking to you now." And the beggar bows to him in affirmation.

The title *Son of man* appears in the gospels 82 times. Perhaps it is significant that Jesus uses it here to underscore his brotherhood with the beggar, his bond with all those ordinary people who may be looked down on by pharisaical eyes but who are loved wholeheartedly by God. Because he is Son of man, Jesus can be wholly one with those who suffer blindness or rejection, paralysis or possession. For him, compassion is never subservient to religious ordinances.

He has come to "make the sightless see and the seeing blind," to divide the true hearts from the pretenders to virtue. Insulted, the Pharisees bluster, "So we are blind, are we?" Jesus gives it to them straight:

> If you were blind
> you would not be guilty.
> But since you say 'We can see,'
> your guilt remains.

A line from *Lear* captures the Pharisees' final state. "So out went the candle, and we were left darkling." It is spoken by the Fool.

> *Lord, forgive us for the times when we have been blind guides with glass eyes and marble hearts.*

*Consider:*

Jesus seems to use "Do you believe in the Son of man?" not only to prompt a declaration of faith, but to differentiate between the blind guides and the farsighted believers. How might you take this question in the context of your present relationship with Jesus?

Do you see and respond compassionately to those who are, in whatever ways, begging for help or guidance? Why or why not?

Do you occasionally fall into the Pharisees' trap of living as though allegiance to religious laws was all that was required of you?

*Act:*

What will you do today as a sign of repentance for any willful blindness you may have practiced in the past?

## *Day 5*   *Why do you not understand what I say?*
*(Jn 8:43)*

*Scripture context: Jn 8: 31-47*

---

Father Ed Hays tells a pungent little tale that was passed on to him by a county attorney in a small Kansas town:

> In a certain jury trial, an old farmer was called to the stand and asked by the judge to swear on the Bible that he would "tell the whole truth and nothing but the truth." The farmer opined as how he'd have to refuse. Asked why by the flabbergasted judge, he said, "Well, your honor, in the first place I don't know if I know the whole truth; and even if I did know the whole truth, I wonder if you or the jury could stand to hear it. So, with your permission, I'll tell you as much of the truth as I think I know, and as much as I think you and the jury can bear to hear." The judge smiled and told him to proceed.

I'd bet my hardbound copy of *The Best of Modern Humor* that the inimitable Storyteller from Nazareth loves this one. He well knows just how little truth we can bear at any one time.

And who knows better the centuries-old arsenal of defensive tactics we employ in any confrontation with a discomfiting truth? Their number includes:

> willful misunderstanding
> sidetracking
> obtuse questioning
> claiming allegiance to tradition
> appealing to a higher authority
> fabricating
> making ad hominem attacks
> plain old dodging and weaving.

Paraphrasing Augustine, we pray, "Lord, show us the truth about ourselves—but not all of it—and not yet."

Once in Jerusalem Jesus was addressing a crowd of Jews who had already accepted him as an inspired teacher and who wanted to hear more. Feeling affirmed by their numbers, he held out to them the pithy core of his teaching, a lustrous pearl that was theirs for the taking.

"If you make my word your home
you will indeed be my disciples;
you will come to know the truth,
and the truth will set you free."

What presumption, they thought. Set them free, indeed. Who did this Jesus think he was? They were the sons of Abraham, the sole possessors of the One True God who had always, even in the Babylonian captivity, jealously guarded their spiritual freedom like a diadem.

Undeterred, Jesus forges ahead, explaining that their succession from the patriarchs does not exempt them from the generic human weakness in temptation nor does it ensure enlightenment. Jews sin just as surely as Samaritans and Phoenicians do. Sin is falsity to the true self, the true God. Only the Son can free them from this ancient slavery. Only by accepting the Son into their daily lives can they experience truth. Their minds closed tight as clams, the Jews burrow into the sand lest they be swept away by the tide of his conviction.

"Why do you not understand what I say?" he asks, knowing the answer but casting out bait. "Because you cannot bear to listen to my words." You cannot bear it. The truth is a difficult language to master. On this particular day the Jews prefer the more familiar native tongue of self-deception. They are not yet ready to disavow their allegiance to the "father of lies."

The irony of their resistance stings Jesus. He has miscalculated their readiness for conversion. And their respect for him as a teacher of the faith seems to have dried up on the vine. They refuse to be budged. Some are already plotting his demise. "He is getting too carried away with himself. This message cannot be swallowed," they murmur, vowing to hear no more of it.

They have, of course, heard none of it. They are constitutionally incapable of doing so now that they have withdrawn into their brittle shells. For his part, Jesus is constitutionally incapable of giving up hope in them. He tries once again to pry them open.

"Whoever comes from God
listens to the words of God;
The reason why you do not listen
is that you are not of God."

Do you hear me, friends? You must live by every word, every truth that comes from God. Not just the ones you already agree with or find inspiring. Not just the ones your fathers and mothers before you accepted. You must be able to live by the truth that requires you to change your ways, to alter your attitudes, to let go of stereotypes. Right now you must accept the truth that demands conversion, that demands that you come out of enslavement to the father of deception.

*Jesus, reveal to us day by day as much of the truth as you think we can bear. And be there to bear it with us.*

*Consider:*

If Jesus asks you today, "Why do you not understand what I say?" are you aware of any word or truth which you have been resisting?

Is there an attitude or a habit that you have not examined in the light of truth?

Is there any teaching of Jesus which you consider too much to bear?

*Act:*

What specific effort will you make to accept a difficult or discomfiting word of God?

# *Day 6*   *Why are you so frightened?* (Mk 4:40)

*Scripture context: Mk 4:33-41*

Whenever I come across the gospel story of the storm at sea, I remember St. Therese of Lisieux. Her application of the narrative is as engaging and ingenious as anything in her "Little Way" to sanctity. The young Carmelite, in reflecting on the story, related not to the terrified disciples but to the exhausted Lord asleep "on a cushion." His goodness and wisdom and healing energy had been siphoned off by a needy crowd. Now the Caretaker wanted to be taken care of. Therese understood. She would have gone silently to the bottom of the sea rather than disturb him.

As she meditated further, Therese envisioned the constant demands to which Jesus was still subjected. Think of all those intercessory prayers battering heaven's gate day after day. "I know that other souls rarely let Him sleep peacefully, and He is so wearied by the advances He is always making that He hastens to take advantage of the rest I offer him," she observed in her autobiographical *Story of A Soul.*

What was the rest she offered? During times of darkness or grief, when prayer was corn-husk dry, she sometimes pictured Jesus asleep in her boat. And she allowed him to slumber on. Like a mother, she protected him at her own expense. While this may sound at first like nothing more than a pious Victorian devotion, in practice it was for Therese an exercise in courage.

One day early in Jesus' itinerant life he had been teaching an immense crowd occupying the seashore at Galilee. From a boat bobbing lightly on the green water, he had shared the story of the sower and many other parables with them. The size of the crowd and the intensity of his delivery exacted a toll which became evident by evening. His voice cracked, his throat ached, his head echoed like an empty well.

"Let us cross over to the other side," he said to his friends, confident that they would get the message. While Peter and Andrew pushed off, Jesus settled himself on the afterdeck with his head on the helmsman's seat. He stretched and yawned expansively. His body settled into the rhythm of the boat and the sea. It was time for the disciples to take over. They were in their natural element. And they too were glad now to leave the multitude behind.

Jesus slept. As often happened on the Sea of Galilee, a sudden storm arose when colder winds came rolling down the embracing hills, gathering menace as they swept across the water. Within minutes, the boat was swamped by waves threatening disaster. The disciples had endured their share of storms. But this one would not let them off lightly. Their boat quickly filled with the agitated sea, sweeping away their manly self-control.

The sight of Jesus sleeping his way through the terror around him provoked the disciples. If he couldn't help them in this calamity, he could at least keep them company and suffer the last few minutes with them. Peter shook the rabbi's shoulder rudely and asked, ''Master, do you not care? We are lost!'' He hadn't intended to put it quite that way but the serenity of Jesus' face had nettled him all the more.

Without bothering to answer Peter's complaint, Jesus stood to confront the despoiler of his much-needed repose. He rebuked the hysterical wind and shushed the sea. His tranquility invaded them and they settled down like ungainly dogs whose barking has been silenced at their master's command.

In the silence, Jesus said to his disciples, ''Why are you so frightened?'' Had he stopped there, they might have come up with a number of plausible suggestions. But he followed through with a second query that negated all the responses they might have made to the first. ''Have you still no faith?'' he inquired, reprimanding them for losing the key to their relationship with him.

No one said a word as Jesus returned to his nap. But as soon as his regular breathing reassured them, they began to whisper to one another, ''Who can this be? Even the wind and the sea obey him.'' In their excitement, they went from one to the other, clasping shoulders and bear hugging, dying to grab Jesus and raise him on their shoulders like David over the vanquished Philistines. But they did not dare rouse him.

For St. Therese, the storm at sea could be any encounter that threatened her equilibrium or engulfed her heart in darkness. It could be something as ordinary as an unresolved misunderstanding with another sister (which, in an enclosed monastery, can be crippling), or as depressing as a week in which every prayer she attempted to skip over the surface of the water fell with a dull kerplunk.

Time and again she endured the turmoil, smiling at the figure of Jesus reclining, asleep yet not unaware. Unlike the disciples in training, Therese was certain that even if the storm capsized her the Lord would rescue her from death. She could trust his mastery of nature as well as his constant care for her.

*So take your rest, gentle Master. But with us who are neophytes
on the mercurial sea, keep one eye open in our direction.*

*Consider:*
   "Why are you so frightened?" Name some of the important ways in which you are afraid to trust Jesus.

Choose one of these fears to work with.

How might you, in a small-step fashion, begin to demonstrate
greater trust in the Lord when these particular storm clouds loom?

*Act:*
   What will you do to make the image of Jesus asleep in your boat
meaningful in your own prayer life?

# *Day 7*  *Why did you doubt?* *(Mt 14:31)*

*Scripture context: Mt 14: 22-33*

---

In her book *Walking on Water*, Madeleine L'Engle mourns the loss of our ability to see angels and to remember how to walk on water. She observes, "God is always calling on us to do the impossible. It helps me to remember that anything Jesus did during his life here on earth is something we should be able to do, too."

Peter was able to step sprightly across the Sea of Galilee until he remembered that mere human beings had long since forgotten how. At that precise moment, the water claimed mastery over him. He no longer believed in his ability to do the impossible.

Lewis Carroll's Queen of Hearts had no such problem. She had, of course, made it a point to practice at least half an hour a day when she was young. "Why sometimes I've believed six impossible things before breakfast," she boasted to Alice. The queen may have carried things a tad too far. But she would have given Peter a run for his money when it came to keeping her head above water.

After feeding the five thousand on the seashore, Jesus sent the people home and urged his companions to sail off to the other side of the lake. Evening, cloaked in sleepy lavender, crooned of the hour for meditation. As soon as Peter pulled ashore, Jesus went up on a hill by himself to pray. He laid down on the cool earth, allowing himself to be held like a child against Yahweh's bosom.

Several hundred feet offshore the disciples too were taking their rest when the rocking of their boat became a wild lurching that tossed them around like hapless flounder. It was three o'clock in the morning. Their sleep-snared heads could hardly cope with the storm's sudden reality.

When a figure came gliding toward them on the water, their apprehension was converted to terror and they cried out, hoping to wake themselves from the nightmare. "It's a ghost!" someone shouted into the waves, his voice quaking.

"Courage! It's me! Don't be afraid!" Jesus directed. How many times would he have to give them that advice? How often would he have to remind them that they had nothing of consequence to fear?

Peter was quick to respond. (Had he been fully awake, he would have thought better of it. But as it was, he strode right in.) "Lord, if it is really you, tell me to come to you across the water," he said, testing but eager to join in the fun. He had already imagined himself out there side by side with his beloved friend, strolling effortlessly over the surface, weightless and invincible.

"Come," Jesus answered, heartened by the disciple's daring. That was all Peter needed. The voice and the image drew him on. He tumbled over the side and began walking toward the Lord. Oh, glory! Oh, the wonder of it! He was a boy and anything was possible. The surface, calmed to a ripple, felt firm beneath his bare feet. He was tall, noble, majestic, free. Jesus was there, smiling encouragement at him, pleased as a father who watches his toddler walk for the first time.

For a second, Peter's attention flickered. He perceived not who he was with but where he was. The shoreline was as distant as the moon. Fright flooded in through his goggling eyes. Flailing desperately, heavy and graceless as a boulder, he began to sink. "Lord, save me!" he cried. "Save me!"

Jesus stretched out his hand and caught Peter by the arm, hauling him up to safety. He had been so elated by his friend's previous performance that now he could not restrain a rebuke. "You have so little faith," he complained. "Why did you doubt?"

Peter, out of breath and out of answers, clung to Jesus as though he would never let him go. Slowly, as they made their way to the boat, he felt the Lord's vitality penetrating his heart, his lungs, his shaking limbs. In this proximity, fear fled the power of Jesus' person. As they climbed aboard, the disciples surrounded them. Their eyes wet with excitement and gratitude, they touched the rabbi reverently, saying, "Beyond doubt you are the Son of God!"

But of course they were not beyond doubt. The day would come when they could see angels and raise the dead, tread on snakes and defy imperial Rome, speak in tongues and walk on water. Meanwhile, they had to come to terms with "Why did you falter?" They had to practice believing that all things are possible to one who loves God.

*Lord, stretch out your saving hand and draw us up out of the sea of uncertainty.*

*Consider:*
Have you ever attempted any act of faith which required you, like Peter, to answer God's call to do the "impossible"?

(The impossible is a highly individual matter. It might mean daring:

to step into an intimidating position of leadership
to be a peacemaker between "warring parties"
to witness to your faith among skeptics
to trust yourself in a relationship.

There are many ways of walking on water.)

How do you hear "Why did you doubt?" and how will you answer?

*Act:*
What will you do at the first opportunity to go beyond any particular "faltering" you have experienced in the past?

# Day 8    *Why do you ask me about what is good?* *(Mt 19:17)*

*Scripture context: Mt 19:16-24*

---

A dialogue overheard between a 15-year-old high school sophomore and her middle-aged but still hopeful mother:

Teen: Mom, I've been thinking what I'd really like to do is go to Harvard Med School.

Mom: That's nice, dear.

Teen: Do you think I could swing it?

Mom: Well, of course, dear. But first you'd have to improve your grades. That means more study time and fewer parties.

Teen: Yeah. I see what you mean.

Mom: Then you'd have to take more science courses during your junior and senior years. Things like microbiology and advanced chemistry.

Teen: Yeah. I guess so.

Mom: Finally, you'd have to get a part-time job any day now so you could begin saving for this major investment.

Teen: Yeah . . . Mom?

Mom: What is it, dear?

Teen: How do you feel about two-year business schools?

As the Earl of Chesterfield once remarked, "Advice is seldom welcome, and those who want it the most always like it the least." Often what we seek is not so much advice as agreement with the views or decisions we have already adopted. We are rarely eager to accept the kind of advice that requires us to face our inadequacies or endanger our present comfort.

A rich young man approached Jesus asking, "Master, what good deed must I do to possess everlasting life?" He had come of his own accord out of obvious respect for Jesus as a wise spiritual guide. Sensing his sincerity, the Teacher began by putting him on his toes, letting him know that theirs was not to be an idle philosophical discussion.

"Why do you ask me about what is good?" he asked. "There is One alone who is good. But if you wish to enter into life, keep the commandments."

There is a dual invitation in the response. First, by his apparent denial of a single identity binding himself and the One who is good, Jesus invites reflection on that identity. (The question has a ring much like the one addressed to Peter: "Who do you say I am?" In that dialogue, Jesus drew from his disciples a declaration of faith that separated them from the crowd with its varied opinions on his identity.) Secondly, he bids the young man to fulfill those laws of divine-human relationship by which God reveals the path to harmonious living.

The young man, missing the first part of the invitation, zeroes right in on the how-to. Which commandments, he wants to know. Jesus accommodates him by quoting five of the commandments directing mutual respect, then adds "Love your neighbor as yourself."

Relieved and pleased with himself, the inquirer says, "I have kept all these; what more do I need to do?" His youthful idealism thirsts for a higher goal. He wants to do not only what is required, but what is desired and praiseworthy. Jesus looks at him with love. Then he opens wide the storehouse of his wisdom and gives the seeker a long look inside.

"If you wish to be perfect," he says "go and sell all your possessions and give the money to the poor. You will then have treasure in heaven; then, come follow me."

The impact of this advice sets the young man back on his heels. He had not thought his idealism would cost him so dear. Sell his possessions? The very possessions he had always been led to believe were a mark of God's favor to him? Who would he be without his possessions? Jesus had given him the answer. But the young man could not accept it. He went away sad for his possessions were many.

Watching the inquirer retreat, Jesus pitied him for his failure to accept either of the invitations he had been offered. He had not truly recognized the Teacher. Nor had he been willing to move on to the next stage in his spiritual journey. He could not imagine the utter goodness of finding his security in the Lord rather than in wealth.

When the young man was no longer in view, Jesus turned and said to his companions, "I assure you only with difficulty will a rich man enter into the Kingdom of God." He glanced down the road one more time. But no one was there.

*Lord Jesus, loosen our grip on whatever possessions prevent us from becoming true disciples.*

*Consider:*

"Why do you ask me about what is good?" Is this Jesus' way of saying to you, "Why do you come to me seeking the path to perfection if, in your heart, you do not fully intend to follow my advice? If I am as good as you say, why not do what I say?"

Identify those possessions that may presently be obstacles to your own discipleship. Focus on one of these in your response.

*Act:*

How will you give to the poor today as a pledge of your lived recognition of Jesus' goodness?

## Day 9 — Why not judge for yourselves what is upright? *(Lk 12:57)*

*Scripture context: Lk 12:54-59*

---

How do you read these signs of the times? Do they offer any direction for the way you lead your daily life?

Every day around the world 40,000 children under the age of five die from hunger, illness and war.

There are now 35.3 million poor people in the United States, the richest country in the world.

The 2.5 billion women in the world receive one-tenth of the world's income. Two-thirds are illiterate.

Forty-five million adults in the world are now unemployed.

Perhaps we shake our heads at the monumental injustice of it all. Maybe we pray the rosary for starving children, or send a donation to Catholic Charities on behalf of the poor. Then what? Should we wait for a study commission report from Washington or an encyclical from Rome to tell us what to do next?

Jesus wasn't good at keeping his cool when it came to preaching on the signs of the times. He could barely fathom how resistant people seemed to be to the most obvious truths that called to them with the insistence of the shofar at sunset on Fridays. Sometimes he even imagined himself prying them loose from their accustomed stances, saying, with barely disguised impatience, "What are you waiting for?"

Speaking to the crowds one day, he decided to throw parables to the winds. He would spell it out for them, baring the message in its most elemental form. "When you see a cloud looming up in the west," he noted, "you say at once that rain is coming, and so it does." They nodded their heads, accompanying him down a familiar path.

"When the wind is from the south you say it's going to be hot, and it is," he added. And the people said, "That's right, rabbi." This lesson was going to be easy. No verbal hooks or unexpected zingers to throw them off balance.

"Hypocrites!" he retorted, without raising his voice one iota. "You know how to interpret the face of the earth and the sky. How is it you do not know how to interpret these times? Why not judge for yourselves what is upright?''

Whack. Wake up! Why are you waiting for me to lead you, step by step, sign by sign? God has given you a brain and five senses to inform it. You have heard my teaching and observed my witness. You have seen me healing, consoling, forgiving. Yet you remain anchored in the bay as though you could not set sail without precise orders from the captain.

Determined to get through to them, Jesus went on to another example. Suppose you are going with an opponent before the magistrate, he said. ''Make an effort to settle with him on the way or he may drag you before the judge and the judge hand you over to the officer and the officer have you thrown into prison. I tell you, you will not get out until you have paid the very last penny.''

Now this is sound practical advice. Not the sort of thing people should need to be instructed on in great detail. Self-interest alone informs them that if they are involved in any conflict, they should be willing to forgive, to compromise, to seize the opportunity for an amiable reconciliation. Otherwise, they may wind up paying through the nose for their failure to respond to the signs of the times.

They may pay in ulcers, insomnia, hurt feelings and heavy grudges. They may pay in broken relationships and lost opportunities to do good, as well as in the vague dissatisfaction induced by guilt ignored. More importantly, they may pay in a just judgment reserved for the day of their death (''Forgive us our sins as we forgive those who sin against us'').

*Lord, prod us to read the signs of the times creatively and without procrastination. Remind us that ''no one told us what to do'' is not a valid excuse for grown-ups.*

*Consider:*

''Why not judge for yourself what is upright?'' What area of your personal or communal life might Jesus be calling your attention to?

Name a sign of the times that you have been ignoring or holding off at arm's length?

Name an injustice (economic, societal or moral) which you have not acted upon because you were waiting for the "opportune time" or for assurance from someone in authority? (Recall that Martin Luther King believed, "The time is always ripe for doing right.")

Be specific in deciding whether and how Jesus' warning may apply to you.

*Act:*

Select either a sign of the times you have ignored in the past or one of those listed in the opening of today's meditation. Respond to it in some generous action within the next few days.

42

## Day 10    *What can we say the kingdom is like?*
*(Mk 4:30)*

*Scripture context: Mk 4:30-34*

---

A friend of mine several years ago brought forth a modest little mimeographed newsletter she called "The Mustard Seed." Naomi's network of friends was loosely flung over half the planet. So she thought it would be a good idea to cast the "Seed" hither and yon, inviting her correspondents in Philadelphia and San Francisco, El Salvador and England, Canada and the Philippines to contribute to its homely pages.

At first it was a few pages long with most of its lively contents cooked up by the editor. (She wasn't exactly new at the game, having been a senior editor for Doubleday and a literary agent for the likes of Thomas Merton.) But ever so gradually, month by month, the subscribers began to make it their own with a green stalk of poetry here and a flowering branch of spiritual direction there.

One issue might accommodate offerings as varied as a Chicago soup kitchen volunteer's SOS for donations, a depressed seminarian's plea for prayer support and a young mother's inspired account of how she recognized God in the contemplative gaze of her infant son.

In a year or so, "The Mustard Seed" was fully grown, eight to ten pages long, sheltering the ideas, hopes, dreams and sufferings of a farflung community. At Christmas all of our names would appear in a symbolic concentric circle design composed with patient care by the founder. When Naomi Burton Stone's schedule dictated her departure from the Seed, we all felt we had been cut off from a place of welcome and nourishment and affirmation—in short, from a spiritual home.

After explaining the parable of the sower to his friends, Jesus told another which he introduced with a double-barreled question. "What can we say the kingdom is like?" he asked. "What parable can we find for it?" Perhaps he meant to be rhetorical or merely introductory.

But there is something inviting about the "we" as Jesus uses it here (unlike the royal or editorial *we* which often enough says "Hush up and listen to my august pronouncement''). Wouldn't it have been like Peter the Outspoken to venture an opinion? How about Thomas who was strong-minded enough to insist on proof before he could fall head over heels in faith? Whatever responses there may have been, we can be sure, are recorded in the memory of the Teacher who loved to draw his disciples out.

Using an earthy example as familiar to his listeners as the ''golden arches'' are to us, Jesus went on to compare the kingdom to a grain of mustard seed which ''when sown upon the ground, is the smallest of all the seeds on earth.'' From the start, he wanted them to conceive of a kingdom not fully grown and splendidly displayed, but a kingdom in embryo, hidden and insignificant, seemingly without promise or potential.

However, what happens to this tiny seed if it is nourished and preserved from the ravages of the heavy foot or the impatience of the premature harvester? ''Yet when it is sown it grows into the biggest shrub of all,'' Jesus reminded them, calling up awareness of the slow and certain growth of the subtle reign of God. The crowd would instinctively recognize this luxuriant tree as a symbol of Yahweh's rule.

Jesus then completed his parable and his sensual picture, saying ''it puts forth big branches, so that the birds of the air can shelter in its shade.'' ''Ah,'' the people must have responded knowingly, seeing the well-rounded mustard tree, heavy with its flamboyant leaves of dark green and multi-petaled blossoms of rich yellow. Congregating there in great numbers, the sparrows took shelter and shade, comfort and companionship.

He said no more, confident that the parable would do its own work in its own time. Let the glory of the kingdom speak to them from the open mouths of mustard blossoms. Let the power of the kingdom whisper to them in the humble seed. Let the promise of the kingdom sing to them in virtuoso bird songs that all sounded like melodies of home.

How he loved the image his parable had conceived! And how much more did he love the immanent reality it signified!

*Jesus, make us patient sowers of mustard seeds that grow into capacious kingdoms where you reign forever and ever. Amen.*

*Consider:*

Hear the question of Jesus as an invitation to enter into dialogue on the key image of his life. He says to you, ''What can we say the kingdom is like?'' (What comparison comes to your mind, teases your imagination, when I say ''kingdom of God''? I'll tell you about my mustard seed if you tell me about your image.)

You might begin by brainstorming—jotting on paper all the images, ideas, words that ring kingdom bells for you.

Choose one of these and develop a comparison between it and the kingdom. Try to create your own parable to share with the Lord as your response to his question.

*Act:*

Decide how you will activate your parable by becoming a more kingdom conscious person.

# Part Two
# Seeking Growth

If we stop at seeking guidance from the scriptures, we remain white-veiled novices hanging around in the convent enclosure rather than striding out the front door to test our resolve. A professed disciple confronts the Bible with her sandals fastened, ready to make tracks. Like Francis of Assisi facing the ulcerated leper in his path, a disciple seeks something more to grow on.

In this regard, Jesus the Questioner never disappoints. It is his nature to pry us out of whatever adolescent refuge we may be loitering in. If we complain that we are giving up prayer because we get such poor results, he tweaks us with a query about a widow who hassles a recalcitrant judge into submission.

If we are inclined to rest on our exemplary record of generosity to family and friends, he shakes us up by inquiring "But what have you done for your enemies lately?"

If we commend ourselves for tirelessly serving the parish, the poor, or the cause of world peace, he yanks the red carpet out from under us by musing aloud about what we have done more than our duty.

He gives us this strong drink to signify that we have come of age. Like the prescient coach who sees a Jim Thorpe in the runner who can't yet clear the hurdles, Christ keeps urging us onward and upward, spurred by his acute vision of our yet-unrealized selves.

Paul caught a glimmering of what drives the Rabbi to keep after us. He explained it to the Ephesians:

> On each of us God's favor has been bestowed in whatever way Christ allotted it. . . . [These gifts are to be used] to knit God's holy people together for the work of service to build up the Body of Christ until we all . . . form the perfect Man fully mature with the fullness of Christ himself. Then we shall no longer be children . . . we shall grow completely into Christ (Eph 4:7, 12-15).

## Day 11  Now, will not God see justice done?
(Lk 18:7)

*Scripture context: Lk 18:1-8*

---

Does the Christian peace activist live who has not taken comfort in the parable of the widow and the judge? Is there a grieving mother of a lost child in Argentina or an illegal alien in California who could not identify with the heroine of this gospel story?

Sister Joan Chittister, OSB, who champions the interrelated causes of peace, justice and women's rights, wrote a column not long ago called "Patient Endurance" ("Pax Christi USA," Winter 1986). Out of her long and frustrating experience as a pleader for the rights of the oppressed, as a petitioner of stern and/or wrongheaded power brokers in church and state, she reminded readers that it is "only by 'patient endurance' that we can save our souls."

The black civil rights marchers of the '60s who kept "their eyes on the prize," the coalition of anti-war demonstrators who persisted until the U.S. withdrew from Vietnam, the volunteers who year after year through Network, Oxfam, the Sanctuary Movement try to change the system, would all say "Amen" to this gospel slogan for survival.

For those who were tempted to lose heart, Sister Joan related the story of an ancient wise person who ran through the streets shouting, "Power, greed and corruption!" In the beginning, people stopped to wonder at his oddball behavior. But they soon turned away and went about their business. One day a child took pity on the wise person and asked, "Don't you realize that no one is listening to you?"

The wise one responded, "Of course I do, child."

"Then why do you keep shouting? If no one is changing, your efforts are useless."

"Oh, no they aren't," the seer concluded. "You see, I do not shout only in order to change them. I shout so that they cannot change me."

Jesus told his disciples a parable on the necessity of patiently enduring in the prayer of word and action. There was in a certain city a corrupt judge who always looked out for Number One. He was a power unto himself, a person moved only by self-interest and greed.

A poor widow in that city had been unable to secure her rights from some well-to-do property owner. So she kept coming to the judge, saying, "I want justice from you against my enemy!" Day after day she reappeared before the magistrate and reiterated her petition. No matter how apathetic he seemed or how much time passed, she persisted.

Finally eroded by her endurance, the judge said to himself, "Even though I have neither fear of God nor respect for any human person, I must give this widow her just rights since she keeps pestering me, or she will come and slap me in the face." (What a fine comic image! The grey-haired widow methodically clubbing the hardheaded judge with her endless entreaties. Take that! And that!)

Jesus, after relishing the picture a bit himself, went on, "You noticed what the unjust judge has to say? (Now pay attention, friends. I have an important question for you.) Now, will not God see justice done to his elect if they keep calling to him day and night even though he still delays to help them?"

Ah, the temptation he dangles before them (and us) in that word "delay." How long, O Lord, will you delay in answering us? How many times must the cannonballs fly before they're forever banned? How many years must we petition for an end to the arms race, to apartheid, to male dominance in church and state, to chemical exploitation of the planet?

"Will not God see justice done?" asks us to consider the ways in which God has already heard the widow's petitions. We are out of Vietnam. The civil rights movement has made astounding progress. Women are sharing more of the world's responsibilities and men are sharing more of the household responsibilities.

The question also prompts us to examine our concept of time, since God's time is not ours. Patient endurance does not come easy to a generation raised on instant mashed potatoes, instant telecommunications, instant gratification via Visa and Mastercard.

Jesus assures his friends, "I tell you, he will give them swift justice." What God sees as swift justice comes after a time of patient endurance, of persistent prayer, of humble supplication, of not losing heart. God's justice comes to those who keep shouting not only to change the world, but to make darn sure that the world does not change them.

*Lord, help me to believe in God's swift justice so that I will never tire of taking the world's case to court.*

*Consider:*

What feelings or reactions does "Will not God see justice done?" arouse in you? Write out these reactions so you can take a good look at them before considering your response to the Lord.

Share some of the ways in which you have persisted—or failed to persist—in seeking justice.

*Act:*

How will you emulate the widow in some small or large way, starting today?

## Day 12 Why does this generation demand a sign? *(Mk 8:12)*

*Scripture context: Mk 8:11-13*

---

J. Anthony Lukas began a *New York Times* book review recently by quoting a remark reportedly made by President Ronald Reagan to a pro-Israeli lobbyist. Said Reagan, ''I turn back to your ancient prophets in the Old Testament and the signs foretelling Armageddon, and I find myself wondering if—if we're the generation that's going to see that come about.'' He went on to add that he was convinced there were biblical end-time signs evident everywhere.

Speculating on whether Reagan wasn't ''predisposed'' toward nuclear war as the final showdown between good and evil, Lukas goes on to praise the paradoxically-titled book *Blessed Assurance: At Home With the Bomb in Amarillo, Texas,* by A. G. Mojtabai. In the book, Mojtabai profiles the hometown of Pantex, the plant where all nuclear weapons built in America are assembled. Through extensive interviews, she discovers that the city's Christians, who support 200 churches there, have also been interpreting heavenly signs. However, they are not disturbed by the prospect of nuclear destruction. Why? Because they believe in ''the Rapture'' by which the righteous will be plucked from the jaws of disaster while conflagration claims the rest.

By dividing the world into good and evil camps, this view leads to a kind of ''apocalyptic fatalism'' which does not allow for mutual trust or negotiation with the enemy, Mrs. Mojtabai observes. End-time Christians, she implies, prefer the certitude of the signs to the risky business of making peace on an imperiled planet. They are more at home with the ''blessed assurance'' of the Rapture than they are with the frustrating struggle involved in helping to build the kingdom for all God's people—not just the elect.

On the very day that Jesus had fed four thousand people by multiplying the loaves and fishes, he had an unwelcome encounter with a group of sign interpreters who were more interested in their own agenda than his depleted condition. They had picked a poor time to confront him. Like the mother of an extended family gathered at the holidays, he had spent himself in the effort to make certain that everyone had enough to eat.

("I feel sorry for all these people; they have been with me three days and have nothing to eat. If I send them home hungry, they will collapse on the way. Some of them have come a great distance." He had to reward their fidelity and sate his own desire to be the liberal host.)

Now he was ready to retire to Dalmanutha, his place of private prayer. But the Pharisees stood before him, adopting a theologically pugilistic stance. Mark's gospel tells us, "They demanded of him a sign from heaven."

These same men had either observed or participated in the miraculous meal. They had seen Jesus healing the sick, giving sight to the blind, exorcising demons. Such miracles were not enough for them. They wanted proof that Jesus was the messiah. They demand some incontestable apocalyptic omen that will convince them, beyond the shadow of a doubt, that Jesus heralds the reign of Yahweh.

Devout Jew that he was, Jesus must have felt his ironic kinship with the Lord God at Massah ("the place of the test") and Meribah ("place of the quarreling") when the Israelites—fresh from the spectacular crossing of the Red Sea and stuffed with the fortuitous manna and quail—tried God's patience by asking, "Is the Lord in our midst or not?" Moses had to produce water from the rock on Horeb as a sign that God was still protecting them.

Jesus' response to the demand of the Pharisees stirs our empathy. "With a profound sigh he said, 'Why does this generation demand a sign? In truth, I tell you no such sign will be given to this generation.'" (Scripture scholars note that this final statement is so emphatic as to mean "May evil befall me if a sign is given to this generation!")

Because they deny Jesus their trust, they are refused a sign. How much easier it would be for the Pharisees if a loud voice from the heavens trumpeted, "Jesus is the Son of God. You can take my word for it. Please." Unlike the anawim who accept the words and works of Jesus as more than ample signs of his identity, the Pharisees see themselves as a select group deserving of extraordinary assurance. If it is not forthcoming, they will neither follow Jesus nor advance his mission.

Not wanting any further proof of their self-righteousness, Jesus gets into the boat and shoves off in the company of those for whom he himself is sign enough.

*Jesus, I place my entire trust in you, requesting no signs, proofs or unlimited warranties.*

*Consider:*
     Explain any way in which ''Why does this generation demand a sign?'' may apply to your faith life?

Do you ever require certain preconditions before activating your trust in the Lord? Explain.

Give examples of times you are more willing to trust in signs and portents than you are in the mission of building God's kingdom?

Is Jesus himself the sign under which your daily decisions are made and priorities are set? If so, tell how.

*Act:*

What will you do to demonstrate your trust in Jesus (and perhaps in those who do his work of peace and justice making)?

# Day 13

Are you not worth much more than they are? (Mt 6:27)

*Scripture context: Mt 6:19-34*

---

Two icons of Christian simplicity:

Dorothy Day is invited to give the commencement address at St. Joseph's College in North Windham, Maine. Does she go out and buy a new dress, or at least something suitable for the occasion? Not on your life. She appears on stage exactly as she would in any Catholic Worker house— wearing a thrift shop "bag sale" suit and pedestrian shoes that have declined beyond respectability. She speaks of Christ's love for the poor. And people are overwhelmed by her beauty.

The Second Vatican Council is in session in Rome. Dorothy Day sails from New York on a freighter. In the Holy City, she takes a small apartment located in a section not frequented by the princes of the church. There she remains praying for the council for several days. She returns home the way she came.

There is no duality in these two transparent scenes. They compel our inner gaze as powerfully as a rose window in a Gothic cathedral. Dorothy did not divide her loyalties between God and Mammon. She made no concessions to society's insistence that we are what we own. The latest fashions, fads, cars, diets, trends meant nothing to her. When she died, her body was placed in a plain pine box she had been using for 40 years as a storage chest. Dorothy Day was single-hearted.

In the Sermon on the Mount, Jesus served his disciples a hearty meal for the road, fortified with all the nourishing guidance they as spiritual athletes would require. The entree was a non-negotiable command to repudiate whatever would divert us from seeking first the reign of God. If a disciple were to adhere faithfully to all the other guidelines while passing this one up with a murmured "No, thank you," he or she would never get off the starting line.

Jesus explicitly warns us against storing up earthly treasure (grain, barns, money, jewels, stocks, cars, material successes, CDs for a rainy day) at the expense of heavenly values. It is not these treasures in themselves that are dangerous, he implies, but the trust we misplace in them—a trust that rightly belongs only to God. "You cannot serve two masters," he bluntly tells us. "You cannot be the slave of God and money." (But, oh how we excel at trying!)

Sensing that his disciples in every generation will exercise all manner of mental gymnastics to weasel their way out of, over or under this directive, Jesus elaborates it into a three-part warning that defies misinterpretation.

"So do not worry; do not say, 'What are we to eat? What are we to drink? What are we to wear?'" He aims at the core of each person's daily anxieties and insists, "Start here. This is where the real battle lies."

Why? Pointing to the birds of the air who are so well cared for, he asks "Are you not worth much more than they are?" His disciples know the right response. But do they, will they live it? It is one thing to intellectualize the futility of worry and the relative insignificance of what's on our plates and our backs. Yet it is a far, far more difficult thing to let go of anxiety about:

Is my job secure? Does the boss dislike me?

How am I going to balance the budget and pay off the IRS? Will my kids have enough to eat if I have to go on welfare or unemployment compensation?

Am I eating all the right foods? Should I go on a Jane Fonda diet, a macrobiotic diet, a low-cholesterol diet or a Scarsdale diet?

Are my clothes out of style? Am I wearing the right thing? Am I dressed for success? Are people sick of seeing me in this same outfit? Do my clothes make me look too old, too young, too fat, too tall, too dull, too conspicuous?

Jesus lets the air out of all these worries by reminding us that it is life itself (I woke up this morning and I am still breathing) that matters. The how of sustaining life should first be entrusted to God and then pursued without undue fuss. The birds of the air go diligently about the business of gathering their daily food supply. But they don't work themselves to exhaustion storing more than they need. Nor do they worry themselves into a peptic ulcer, asking, "Where will tomorrow's seeds come from? Will some chippy little sparrow get more than me?"

It bears repeating. We cannot give ourselves to God and money. What we can do is live simply enough to evade unnecessary "needs" (like a new dress for the commencement speech, or a first-class ticket to Rome, or a satin-lined casket) to evade the false sense of control and responsibility worry engenders. Simplicity also allows us to evade the embrace of Mammon who squeezes out every ounce of energy, leisure time and skill we can muster, leaving only a few paltry leftovers for the care of kingdom values.

*Jesus, keep those warnings coming while we learn to be single-hearted, learn to be free.*

*Consider:*
What honest answers does your present lifestyle give Jesus when he asks ''Are you not worth much more than they are?''

What answers would you like to be able to give?

*Act:*
How will you let go of one small worry you have been clutching about income, food or clothing?

## Day 14

*For if you love those who love you, what reward will you get? (Mt 5:46)*

*Scripture context: Mt 5:43-48*

---

At an age when most people would be sipping the mulled wine of their dotage and spoiling their great-grandchildren, Lillian and Leonard Luttrell were still adding to their extensive family. The Augusta, Maine couple began sponsoring Vietnamese and Cambodian refugees in 1975 through their Diocesan Human Relations Services.

By 1986, the elderly but hardly retiring Luttrells had parented 36 Southeast Asian families numbering over 100 persons. They had guided, chaperoned, consoled, transported and otherwise helped 100 strangers from a foreign land. Most of the newcomers were non-English speaking and non-Christian. These considerations were as significant to the sponsors as an outdated weather report.

A young refugee resettlement officer, edified by the Luttrells' rarified generosity, observed that they were definitely not suffering from "compassion fatigue." (The term implies an inability to sustain a caring response after repeated exposure to the plight of refugees, the starving or any other disadvantaged group. It is, the experts say, the explanation for the failure of many Christians to volunteer their services or resources.)

Although the Luttrells could well claim a bona fide cause for "compassion fatigue," they have continued to open their hearts to the refugees. They've never said, "Now we've done enough. Charity, after all, begins at home. We have our own family to think about." Lillian and Leonard have made no distinction between their natural offspring and their spiritual sons and daughters from afar. They have heard Paul's advice to the Romans ("Have the same attitude toward all") and they have grown into the maturity of compassion.

A primary but little practiced theme of the Sermon on the Mount is "Love your enemies." Contrasted with the terms *neighbor* or *countryman* (as in "You have heard the commandment, 'You shall love your countryman but hate your enemy'" Mt 5:43), *enemy* can also refer to strangers and aliens, according to the *Jerome Biblical Commentary* (p. 73, Vol. II). Jesus, it seems to me, uses the term in its most comprehensive sense.

"But I say this to you: Love your enemies, and pray for those who persecute you," he says. To so emphatically embody compassion is to give evidence—not just lip service—that we are daughters and sons of our heavenly Father, "for he causes his sun to rise on the bad as well as the good, and he sends down rain to fall on the upright and the wicked alike." Jesus holds up a measuring rod of god-like impartiality and challenges his friends to stretch with the tops of their heads for the goal.

Those who took him at his word must have kept a respectful silence while assuring themselves that what he needed was a nice long rest in the country somewhere away from the pressures that had pried him loose from his moorings. Who could treat an enemy with the same regard shown to a friend? Who could welcome a stranger with the enthusiasm reserved for a relative? How was it possible to be as kind to the unjust as to the just one? Come now, Jesus. Be reasonable.

No doubt the rabbi read their faces, for he went on, moving the issue closer to home. Trapping them in the strait of his righteousness, he asked, "For if you love those who love you, what reward will you get? Do not even the tax collectors do as much?" It was an easy but assertive uppercut that landed squarely on their glass jaws. ("Well, gee, Lord, since you put it like that. . .")

Who could contest him? Why indeed should they commend themselves for doing what came naturally to those who hadn't a shred of faith or a tatter of respectability? And why should God compensate them for returning the love others gave them? Is a child rewarded for eating his favorite candy?

"And if you save your greetings for your brothers," Jesus went on, "are you doing anything exceptional? Do not even the gentiles do as much?" For an Israelite to be compared to a Roman or a Philistine would be an outright insult. Yet it would nail down the truth in Jesus' questions. The disciples were no better than the unbelievers when they showed hospitality only to their own kind. If their faith did not enlarge their hearts and ennoble their actions, how valuable was it?

"You must therefore," Jesus concluded, "set no bounds to your love, just as your heavenly Father sets no bounds to his."

To be perfectly mature in spirit, a disciple must grow into an adult compassion that treats friends and enemies, relatives and strangers, with an undiscriminating care. It doesn't happen overnight. But in beautiful golden-age people like Lillian and Leonard Luttrell, the compassion of Christ lives on in inexhaustible profusion.

*Rabboni, remind me that if my charity does not reach beyond my own hearth I will remain trapped in perpetual adolescence.*

*Consider:*

"For if you love those who love you, what reward will you get?" Allow this question to stir up a brief examination of conscience: Do I spend most of my spare time exclusively with my family and other loved ones?

Do I spend most of my extra money on my family and relatives (to the exclusion of those in greater need)?

Do I ever offer hospitality to those who are not relatives and friends?

Am I making any effort to love someone who does not love me in return (possibly within my family)?

When I see the poor, the refugee, the hungry and the abused on TV, do I take refuge in "compassion fatigue" and do nothing?

How will you respond to Jesus on this difficult question?

*Act:*

Be compassionate today in whatever circumstances you find yourself. Write a prayer asking for the Lord's help in loving with "God-like impartiality."

## Day 15

### If you lend to those from whom you hope to get money back, what credit can you expect? (Lk 6:34)

*Scripture context: Lk 6:27-35*

---

If the IRS were to review your financial records for the past five years, would they find ample evidence to convict you of being a charitable Christian?

For instance, would your checking account testify to your inveterate generosity to the poor, the sick, the peace and justice makers?

Would your savings account (or lack thereof) be a reliable witness to the fact that you do not place all your trust in CDs?

The ministry of money is unexplored territory for many of us. As long as we aren't ducking the Sunday collection basket or ignoring the Salvation Army bell ringers, we may assume that all is well. Catholic pastors (at least those who value their popularity) avoid preaching about money as carefully as Catholic parents evade honest discussion about the facts of life. A number of us have grown up thinking that money—other than that given to the church—played a bit part in our spiritual development.

A dialogue between St. Peter, on night duty at the pearly gates, and a candidate for admission who is hoping to squeak by might go like this:

Peter:  Let's see now. How have you used the money entrusted to your care?

Candidate:  Money? What's that got to do with it? Don't you want to hear about how I rarely missed Mass on holy days of obligation, and almost never practiced artificial birth control unless it was absolutely necessary? Don't tell me you're going to change the rules in the middle of the game.

Peter:  Don't get hyper. Your loyalty to church teachings will be duly registered. I still need to know about your money.

Candidate:  I don't get it. Father O'Riley never asked me about that one in confession.

Peter: You see, my friend, how you handled your money speaks volumes about who you are.

Candidate: Funny. I never thought of it like that.

Peter: I know. Take a few minutes to fill out this survey form. Then we'll see where we stand.

Candidate: *(reading aloud)* "Number one: What percentage of your weekly income have you shared with those in need (outside your own family)?" Geez! Could we change that to "annual income?" *(Peter says nothing.)* "Number two: How often—and how cheerfully—did you lend money without charging interest or requiring repayment?" The Bible doesn't say anything about that. *(Pause)* Does it? *(Silence)* "Number three: How often did you share your money in ways that would multiply the benefits for those in need?" This is getting rough, St. Peter, your holiness. I don't think I can pass it.

Peter: Don't worry. It's not an entrance exam. Just an eye-opener for those who missed the point. We keep hoping each new generation will get the message of "In God We Trust." So far it's been a slow process. Pull up a chair and we'll talk about it.

Continuing with his discourse on the mountain, Jesus extended his antithetical description of the disciples versus the sinners by raising the subject of money. As always, his teaching would propel them beyond the mere observance of a familiar law. He wanted them to know that what they did with the contents of their leather money bags was of no small interest to the Almighty.

The disciples had been raised to treat their kinsmen and neighbors as a privileged group which excluded foreigners (all who were not Jews). They had been instructed by the Book of Deuteronomy to "freely lend to your kinsmen in need" during each sabbatical year.

While debts to fellow Jews were to be relaxed during this seventh year, foreigners might conscientiously be pressed to pay up in full, or "exploited" (see Dt 15:2-3,8). This preferential treatment also applied to charging interest on any kind of loan. Relatives paid no interest; outsiders did (see Dt 23:20).

Jesus' friends were probably still shaking their heads over "doing good to those who do good to you" (You mean we aren't building up our heavenly accounts by cowtowing to our domineering mothers-in-law and taking care of our incontinent grandparents in our own homes?). But he didn't pause for intermission before adding: "If you lend to those from

64

whom you hope to get money back what credit can you expect?" (Uhuh. Now I suppose he wants us to lend to every deadbeat on the block—not to mention those from across the border.)

Aloud, of course, they said nothing, regarding him with reluctant admiration. "Even sinners lend to sinners," he reminded them, "to get back the same amount." In their hearts, they knew he was right.

What was so laudatory about lending your neighbor the money to feed his kids or to patch her roof, when that same sum would later come back to you with grateful acknowledgements? Why should you feel like a prince when you had done nothing more than to temporarily share what was yours only by the grace of God in the first place?

And was it not even less praiseworthy to lend to a foreigner who was down on his luck when you fully expected to make a profit in interest on your loan? Where was God in these transactions? Were you doing anything more than good business?

Their imaginations began to play with Jesus' question, devising situations in which they might lend ten farthings or five bushels of wheat, and when the debtor inquired about the due date and rate of interest, they could enigmatically stroke their chins and say, "We'll see about that when the time comes."

The time, naturally, would never come. The debtor would eventually realize that he or she was really a recipient who owed no more than thanks—and the responsibility of being equally generous in turn. The lender would revel in the joy of being beneficent, not forgetting to be grateful to God for his or her own comparative wealth. Their eyes narrowed as they chuckled knowingly to one another at the wisdom of the rabbi. They were reminded that no area of their lives would remain untouched by the teaching of Jesus. And they were glad of it.

*Lord, prod us to lend liberally, to give gladly, and to thank heaven that we can do both.*

*Consider:*

"If you lend to those from whom you hope to get money back, what credit can you expect?" Hear this question as an invitation to reflect on your attitudes and practices regarding money.

Begin by recalling any times when you lent money or valued possessions to someone in need, without requiring either interest or repayment.

What enabled you to lend so generously in these instances? What
prevents you from lending liberally or giving gladly—especially to
those beyond your immediate family?

What feelings does this question of Jesus arouse in you? Why?

*Act:*
   Choose one of the three questions from "St. Peter's Survey" to
respond to in action this week. Ideas: Decide to tithe weekly for a
particular missioner or give a generous amount to an organization
that enables the hungry to feed themselves.

## Day 16    *Why do you observe the splinter in your brother's eye?* (Lk 6:41)

*Scripture context: Lk 6:39-42*

---

There was once a Christian bookseller who was blessed with success and the loyal services of a first-class secretary. Over the years the bookseller had often shown his appreciation to his secretary by taking her out to dinner, buying her little gifts, and sending her flowers on Valentine's Day.

Now the bookseller had a faithful wife, three children and a house in the suburbs. One evening, when he came home late after having a drink with his secretary, he found his wife entertaining an old college buddy who had dropped by to see him. Although he was pleasant enough while the visitor remained, the bookseller lit into his wife as soon as they were alone.

"What kind of wife are you?" he demanded. "Didn't it occur to you that you should have asked him to come back when I was home? Were you trying to make a play for him behind my back? What do you suppose the neighbors thought? How do you expect me to trust you after this?"

Verily I say unto you, the bookseller was an old hand at the ancient game of self-defense known as projection. Instead of owning his faults he projected them onto others where he could safely—and righteously—revile them.

Likewise, a person who subconsciously despises her own laziness will vehemently criticize another for lack of ambition. One who knows his prayer life is a sham will accuse another of being insincere in his faith. Projection provides a convenient, comfortable and self-absolving technique for living with our sinfulness.

The world's greatest psychologist and spiritual director often spoke as though he were an ophthalmologist. He was keen on curing blindness and other handicaps to sight. To be a "blind guide" was, in Jesus' view, to be sorely afflicted indeed. He was partial to expressions like "Do you see?", "Have you understood?" and simply "Look!"

After alerting his friends to the easily-overlooked applications of "Love your enemies," Jesus went on to raise another point which must have jabbed even the best-defended consciences in his congregation. He knew how myopic they were on this particular point. So he made a deft incision with a query sharp as a surgeon's knife, "Why do you observe the splinter in your brother's eye and never notice the great log in your own?"

A few disciples laughed nervously at the oddity of his hyperbole. "What do you mean by that, rabbi?" they asked, remarking to themselves, "He has a way with words alright. If only I could follow them without stumbling over my own feet all the time."

Jesus obliged them. "How can you say to your brother, 'Brother, let me take out that splinter in your eye' when you cannot see the great log in your own?" He paused, assessing the amount of light that seemed to be penetrating their closed lids. Most were still resisting the surgeon's intrusion.

"Hypocrite," he said, purposely using a pejorative he usually reserved for the Pharisees. "Take the log out of your own eye first, and then you will see clearly enough to take out the splinter in your brother's eye."

That final twist made the operation a success for all those who dared the consequences of improved vision. Before the sun set that day, they began the laborious process of log removal so that someday they might be clear-sighted enough to advise a brother or sister who came to them, complaining, "I've got something in my eye. Can you see it?"

> *Lord, make me as perceptive in seeing my own sins as I think I am in focusing on the faults of others.*

*Consider:*
> "Why do you observe the splinter in your brother's eye?" Examine the possible motives behind the habitual judgments you make of friends, family, co-workers, competitors, strangers. In which cases might these motives correspond with hidden faults, fears or weaknesses of your own?

Begin by listing some of the splinters you have noted in the eyes of others (examples: vanity, greed, envy, sexual infidelity, hypocrisy).

Name the splinters that might be logs in your own eyes. Then choose one and tell why that might be so.

How will you respond to Jesus in reference to this fault or sin?

*Act:*

Today when you hear yourself pointing out, verbally or mentally, the splinter in another's eye, stop. Focus on the log (named above) in your own eye and take one step toward its removal.

# Day 17
### Which of these three, do you think, proved himself a neighbor? (Lk 10:36)

*Scripture context: Lk 10:25-37*

---

The scene lives with the force of an ancient parable in my memory. In a marathon movie, dense with meaning, the encounter of Gandhi with the Hindu father of a Moslem-murdered son still emerges as an ethical diamond.

Gandhi, weakened by yet another fast as nonviolent protest, is resting on a rooftop in Calcutta, surrounded by his friends. He has vowed not to eat until the vicious fighting between Moslems and Hindus stops.

A tall, dark-skinned man with the obsessed look of one who has narrowly escaped shipwreck confronts Gandhi and says, "I am going to hell." Asked why, he explains that in retaliation for his own son's death he has killed an innocent Moslem child. The Mahatma considers the tormented man before him. He then says, "I know a way out of hell."

The father's eyes betray a tiny point of hope as he awaits the wise one's counsel. However, he is hardly prepared for the impact of what he is about to hear. Find another child, Gandhi tells him. Take him into your own home and raise him as your son. "Just be sure that he is a Moslem and that you raise him as a Moslem," he concludes.

For a moment, the man looks as though he could throttle Gandhi on the spot. He is horrified, incensed, revolted. The gnarled roots of hatred between Hindus and Moslems, so prominent a part of his heritage, threaten to pull him further down into antipathy.

But slowly Gandhi's truth wrenches the remorseful father free. He agrees to accept a child of the enemy into his own home.

The sheer power of this vignette may be evident only to those who saw the movie and felt the hatred between India's two major religious groups. If we were to draw a parallel story in which a devout Catholic parent was asked to raise the child of an aggressive anti-Catholic fundamentalist preacher like Jimmy Swaggart and to raise him in his father's image, we would be a long way from the depth of division Gandhi was trying to heal.

Christ-like, he was asking the Hindu father for the greatest proof of love he could give.

When a certain lawyer, intent on making himself look good, inquired of Jesus "Master, what must I do to inherit eternal life?" the Teacher responded with another query. "What is written in the Law? What is your reading of it?" The lawyer then dutifully recited the biblical Law of Love, and Jesus commended him for knowing that he should love God above all and his neighbor as himself.

"And who is my neighbor?" inquired the lawyer, quite sure that he knew the answer. He was somewhat nonplussed when the Teacher gave him not a legally-exact response, but a provocative little story about a Jew who got ambushed on the road to Jericho. It seems that the victim's pitiable condition failed to arouse either a priest or a Levite, both of whom scurried on by.

Now the lawyer was listening intently, and passing instant judgment on these two official representatives of his fellow Jews. Jesus' next line, therefore, hit the lawyer like a magistrate's misplaced gavel.

"But a Samaritan traveller who came on him was moved with compassion when he saw him." ("A Samaritan!" the lawyer thought. "What would a dirty heretic like that care about an Israelite? In fact, he would laugh in the unfortunate victim's face.")

The storyteller went on, knowing full well the ages-deep enmity between the "pureblood" Jews and "mixed-blood" Samaritans whose Israelite ancestors had intermarried with occupying Assyrians and other unbelievers. "He went up to him and bandaged his wounds, pouring oil and wine on them. He then lifted him onto his own mount and took him to an inn and looked after him." On the following day, added Jesus, the Samaritan offered to pay all the expenses of the Jewish victim.

Looking the lawyer in the eye, Jesus asked, "Which of these three, do you think, proved himself a neighbor to the man who fell into the bandits' hands?"

Caught and held like a butterfly on a pin, the lawyer begrudgingly responded, "The one who showed pity towards him." In a voice that said "I rest my case," Jesus concluded, "Go, and do the same yourself."

There was no escaping the implications of "the same." To qualify as a neighbor in God's eyes, the lawyer would have to demonstrate wholehearted compassion (not just peremptory care) toward someone in need, someone he had formerly considered an enemy.

It was not a simple matter of charity to the poor or the sick. The Master required more than that. He required a free decision not only to help a member of a hated group, but to love him like a brother or raise him like a son.

*Lord, teach us to honor the Good Samaritan by the vigor of our compassion toward those who seem to be our adversaries. Amen and amen.*

*Consider:*
"Which of these three, do you think, proved himself a neighbor?" List the various implications about love and compassion that you find in both Gandhi and the Good Samaritan.

Recall any opportunity you have had to be a neighbor to an adversary. How did you respond? Why?

How do you think Jesus might be asking you to live this parable right now?

*Act:*

Begin looking today for an opportunity to make a Good Samaritan commitment to some one or some group to whom you are not naturally connected or attracted.

## *Day 18*  Must he be grateful to the servant?
(Lk 17:9)

*Scripture context: Lk 17:5-10*

Carlo Carretto, in *Letters from the Desert,* recalls his early years before he joined the Little Brothers of Jesus. He had been a leader of Italian youth movements and Catholic Action during World War II. Impressed with his many responsibilities, and with the praise he received from ecclesiastical officials, Carretto had an image of himself in which the pillars of the church stood on his shoulders. He was an indispensable servant of the Lord.

One night in a dream he saw himself withdrawing from the pillars. To his chagrin, nothing happened. The church remained upright. Others took his place, and the world continued on its appointed rounds. Carretto was disappointed, relieved and humbled by this unsuspected reality. That was the moment at which he began to understand the identity of a servant.

Who of us in ministry does not complain of our responsibilities? Yet how many of us think seriously of letting them—along with the gratitude and admiration they so often entail—go? Despite our complaints about a lack of time for prayer and leisure, we often cling to our public identity as selfless, hardworking, indispensable servants of the Lord.

Then one day a dream, a criticism, an illness, a replacement, or some other intrusion forces us to confront the truth. We begin to realize that a pedestal is no place for a servant, and that the Master is the only one whose absence the church could not survive. Maybe we even begin to sort out some of our well-disguised motives for serving, so that we will not mistake a leader's scarlet mantle for a laborer's olive-drab coveralls.

Jesus told his disciples a parable that went something like this: Suppose a certain man had a servant who was out plowing the wheat fields or herding the sheep. When the servant came in from the fields, would the master rush out to greet him, hustle him into the dining room and serve him a six-course meal while commending him for carrying out his many responsibilities?

The disciples chuckled and slapped their knees at this improbable scenario. Jesus then went on to speculate that it was more likely that the master would tell the servant to don his apron, prepare the master's supper, wait on him at table, and then the servant could appease his own hunger.

Nodding, the disciples indicated "That sounds more like it."

Jesus then leaned toward them, eyeing them like a wily fishmonger who knew he would get his price. "Must he be grateful to the servant for doing what he was told?" he asked, choosing his words with care. The master may, indeed, be thankful. But can the servant *expect* his gratitude and his "Well dones"?

"So with you who hear me," the rabbi concluded. "When you have done all you have been told to do, say 'We are useless servants; we have done no more than our duty.'"

Some of them—Peter, James and John especially—were a bit put out by this hard saying. They had come to think of themselves as commendable servants on whom Jesus relied to keep the nomadic community on track. They were primarily responsible for acquiring food and shelter, getting out advance word of the rabbi's arrival, and organizing local volunteers to help with the sick and the handicapped who had come to be healed. Jesus was no administrator. Where would he be without their help? Wouldn't things fall apart without them? Did he really consider them useless servants?

For each of them the day would come when they saw for themselves how dispensable and blessedly insignificant they were as pillars of the apostolic community. They would see that the true servant labors not for privilege nor praise. He or she never takes off the apron, sits down at the table and announces, "Master, I have earned my reward."

*Lord, may we recognize the ways in which we too are useless servants.*

*Consider:*

"Must he be grateful to the servant?" Name some of the ways in which you are the servant of the Lord.

Next to each ministry, note the primary reasons why you are willing to serve in that way. (Be brutally honest, with equal time for the altruistic and the egotistical motives.)

Record as many ways as you can think of in which you are rewarded for your servanthood.

How do you feel about "We have done no more than our duty"? Why?

*Act:*
    Look for an opportunity to serve where your labor will either be taken for granted or done anonymously. (If you are already serving in such circumstances, decide to be more grateful for this path to holiness.)

## Day 19    For who is the greater, the one at table or the one who serves? *(Luke 22:27)*

*Scripture context: Luke 22:24-30*

---

The summer of my senior year in high school I plummeted overnight from the academic heights to the economic pits. One day I was seated at the head table, sampling an epicurean selection of scholarships, honors and awards. The very next morning I was learning the ropes as a split-shift six-days-a-week waitress at a downtown restaurant favored by tourists.

In no time at all, my self-image underwent a sea change. The confidence, pride and affirmation of being a privileged upperclassman was wiped out as easily as a catsup stain on my white nylon apron. I became the anonymous, anxiety-laden, overworked and under-tipped "Oh, miss!" who waited on hundreds of people, week after week, with little or no recognition that I was anything more than an automaton in a hairnet and Red Cross shoes.

It was a summer to forget. But I haven't. There's something that sneaks up on us when we "recline at table," a subtle conviction of superiority over the one who "takes our order" and wears out her (or his) leather soles in pursuit of our dining pleasure. A crackerjack waitress can make us feel like Queen for a Day. But who do we make her feel like?

When Jesus challenged his disciples with the image of the "useless servant," he knew that would not be the last word he ever had to utter on the subject. Eager as they were to serve him, the Twelve did not see themselves as cut out to wait on every other table in town. Even at the Last Supper, with the Lord's shocking servanthood laid out before them, they still couldn't resist a friendly little family dispute about "who should be regarded as the greatest."

Jesus, loving his friends more than ever, despite their painful frailties, gave them an example he knew they could latch onto. "Among the gentiles it is the kings who lord it over them, and those who have authority over them are given the title Benefactor," he said. (He alone in the room could fully appreciate the irony of the latter appellation. Those who enjoyed all the benefits of rank and wealth also received the honor of being known as the patrons of the poor who waited upon them. This was the kind of honor his followers pined for.)

"With you," he said emphatically, "this must not happen." They were not to lord it over others who were younger or poorer or less privileged than they were. Among true disciples, the leader must behave as the servant of all. To be the greatest is to be the lowliest.

"For who is the greater," he asked, "the one at table or the one who serves?" Surely they knew from experience that the one who sits on his duff and orders his roast lamb well-done with just a dollop of mint jelly on the side is better than the poor schnook who runs back and forth balancing 25-pound trays above the heads of the diners.

"Yet," he added, in that characteristic signal of an inversion to come, "here I am among you as one who serves!"

He was wearing a towel wrapped around him like a bottle washer's apron when he said it. It was an image to remember. And they did.

*Jesus, make us more eager to wait at table than to lord it over those who do.*

*Consider:*
    "For who is the greater, the one at table or the one who serves?" Jesus is inquiring here about your understanding of his identity as well as your own.

Do you at times consciously identify with the Lord when you are the one who serves (rather than reclines)?

Recall one experience in which you knew—from the inside—why Jesus chose to serve. Describe it briefly.

What obstacles (of personality, upbringing, state of life) are you aware of that block full acceptance of the servant's identity?

What might you do about these obstacles?

*Act:*

From among your family, work or church relationships, choose a situation where you would be expected to "recline at table" (assume a privilege of some kind). Be a servant instead.

## Day 20    Do you suppose I am here to bring peace on earth? *(Lk 12:51)*

*Scripture context: Lk 12:49-53*

---

Writing homilies is by far the best way to be converted by them. As a contributor to a homiletic service, I've often been surprised, challenged and changed by the final version of my own reflections on the assigned scripture readings. (As E.M. Forster put it, "How do I know what I think until I see what I say?") In the process of moving from rough draft to the revised version, which takes into account the critiques of several editors, I clarify and come to grips with what God's word means to me.

Several years ago I was laboring over a projected homily on 1 Kings 19:19-21 (The call of Elisha) and Matthew 12:46-50 (Jesus and his family). The gospel message of allegiance to God before family ("Who is my mother?. . .") seemed to be underscored by Elijah's reprimand to Elisha when the former calls the latter to follow him as Yahweh's prophet. (Elisha wants to rush home for a farewell celebration with his parents before his unexpected departure. Elijah curtly responds, "Go, go back; for have I done anything to you?" It sounds like, "God Almighty himself calls you and all you can think of is running home to kiss your Mommy and Daddy!")

When the critics responded, I was at first confounded and then delighted with the irony of their divergent views. The three lay editors agreed with my interpretation that we are called to be faithful to God—even in those rare instances where fidelity requires us to turn our backs on our families.

The two priest editors, who had left home and family to follow the Lord, took issue with the homily. They suggested a less radical approach that did not place the listener at odds with his or her spouse, children, parents and in-laws. Understandably, they did not want to threaten domestic peace in homes where it might already be a rarity.

In a series of instructions to his disciples, Jesus caused more than the usual consternation by brandishing three disturbing images of division. Luke records them hard on the heels of the parable of the faithful servant with its slightly ominous conclusion, "When someone is entrusted with a great deal, of that person even more will be expected."

First, the rabbi raised up an image of conflagration. "I have come to bring fire to the earth, and how I wish it were blazing already!" The zealots among the disciples must have taken heart, sniffing the acrid odor of military violence and vengeance.

Although Jesus declined to explain himself, the more reflective listeners guessed that he was referring to the fire of God's word which must be enkindled in every heart if the nation is to be converted. "For Yahweh your God is a consuming fire, a jealous God" (Dt 4:24).

Next the rabbi spoke of baptism as though it were a fiery death rather than a watery renewal. "There is a baptism I must still receive," he said, "and what constraint I am under until it is completed!"

How often before the fire by night he had told them of his baptism by John in the Jordan. They knew it to be the greatest and most glorious day of his life, the day on which a familiar voice from heaven had openly proclaimed, "You are my Son; today have I fathered you."

So why did he now speak with dread of another baptism that burned in the pit of his stomach, binding him like a sentence of death? (At this point, they knew nothing of the suffering he intuited or how it would cleanse the world.)

Jesus then asked, in a tone that seemed to mock their pale aspirations, "Do you suppose I am here to bring peace on earth?" (Well, now that you mention it, Lord, that is what we had in mind—peace, freedom, contentment, security, the good life.) Reading their mystified faces, he went on, "No, I tell you, but rather division. For from now on, a household of five will be divided, three against two and two against three. . ."

His uncompromising word would set father against son and mother against daughter, brother against sister, mother-in-law against son-in-law, first cousin against third cousin. Whoever would purchase domestic peace at the price of his or her discipleship did not know the meaning of peace.

Seeing him at that moment, his eyes afire with conviction, his friends would never again be able to conceive of peace as a downy creature feeding on the kernels of compromise and half measures.

His peace was a solid glowing coal of commitment to God's kingdom, the very commitment that consumed Jesus himself.

*Lord, draw us closer to the compelling fire of your peace!*

*Consider:*

"Do you suppose I am here to bring peace on earth?"
Write an impromptu response to Jesus, telling him of the ways in
which your faith in him has proven to be a cause of division or dissension.

Name one way in which you have tried to "keep the peace" in your
family or your parish or community at the expense of your commitment to God's word as you understand it.

Does Jesus' question call you to a different response? Why?

*Act:*

Do something positive (even daring) today to live up to a particular word of God on which you have compromised in the past out of
a desire to keep the peace.

# Part Three
# Seeking Glory

Guided and grown, in recurring sequence, we come again to the Bible's gate, this time seeking glory. No need to ask the price. Not one of the four gospels makes a secret of it.

The price is renunciation of attachments: "And everyone who has left houses, brothers, sisters, father, mother, children, or land for the sake of my name will receive a hundred times as much, and also inherit eternal life" (Mt 19:29).

The price is renunciation of sleepwalking: "So stay awake, because you do not know when the master of the house is coming, evening, midnight, cockcrow, or dawn; if he comes unexpectedly, he must not find you asleep" (Mk 13:35-36).

The price is renunciation of self: "If anyone wants to be a follower of mine, let him renounce himself and take up his cross every day and follow me" (Lk 9:23).

The price is suffering—if only for a time, only as a prelude: "In all truth I tell you, you will be weeping and wailing. . . . you will be sorrowful, but your sorrow will turn to joy" (Jn 16:20).

Jesus' questions now become more urgent, more insistent. The answers he requires have "faithful" written all over them. Will we share his cup? Face his fears and ours? Watch with those who sweat blood in the bowels of the night? Bear witness to the truth before the police armed with clubs? Love him better than life?

These are the hard, bitter, biting, threshing-chaff-from-wheat questions none of us wants to answer—not in our flesh, not where we live. But there they are, like a ringing in the ears that we try to ignore by turning up the TV or the mental tapes. Fear warns us that in answering we sign a death warrant of a sort. And will Christ be there to walk the gangplank with us?

No Christian writer ever conveyed in more excruciating accuracy this primal horror of suffering without solace than the Jesuit priest Gerard Manley Hopkins. If Christ on the cross had expressed himself in poetic imagery rather than the Seven Last Words, he might have said,

> ..................... And my lament
> Is cries countless, cries like dead letters sent
> To him that lives alas! away.
>
> I am gall, I am heartburn. God's most deep decree
> Bitter would have me taste, my taste is me;
> Bones built in me, flesh filled, blood brimmed the curse.
>
> ("I wake and feel the fell of dark")
>
> O the mind, mind has mountains: cliffs of fall
> frightful, sheer, no-man-fathomed. Hold them cheap
> May who ne'er hung there.
>
> ("No worst there is none")
>
> Why do sinners' ways prosper? and why must
> Disappointment all I endeavor end?
> Wert thou my enemy, O thou my friend,
> How wouldst thou worse, I wonder, than thou dost
> Defeat, thwart me?
>
> ("Thou art indeed just, Lord")

The poet, nailed to the wood of desolation, having answered all Christ's final questions with his vowed life, makes his own justified inquiries. He wonders how his suffering could be any worse if Christ were his bosom enemy instead of his beloved friend.

His only response is a startling cry in the darkness, "*Eloi, eloi, lama sabachthani?*"

## Day 21   *Do you want to be well again?* *(Jn 5:6)*
*Scripture context: Jn 5:1-9*

Pilgrims to Lourdes, their bodies often buckled or flattened by illness, line up outside the baths each day, waiting their turn to be immersed in the glacial spring waters. "Go and drink at the spring and wash in it," the Blessed Lady instructed Bernadette in an 1858 apparition. Emulating the unquestioning young shepherdess, contemporary pilgrims do as they have been instructed, accepting the queues and the waiting as part of their petitioners' identity. There are a limited number of baths and volunteer attendants who help the afflicted in and out of the stone tubs.

Although the Lady promised no cures, about 10,000 pilgrims have reportedly been healed of physical ailments since the Lourdes Medical Bureau opened over a century ago. The last official miracle was proclaimed in 1976. Vittorio Micheli had been told by his doctors that pelvic cancer would end his life within a few days' time. The young Italian insisted that he be taken to Lourdes where he prayed with absolute certainty in the baths. When he emerged, his body began to regenerate bone tissue that had been destroyed by cancer. A month later, Micheli was well again.

A Marist priest who led pilgrims to Lourdes for 20 years says, "About 90 percent of the people who come here hope to be cured. Maybe 100 percent are helped—even though most are not cured." Father Donald Gagne, S. M., former director of the Lourdes Center in Boston, rarely speaks of miracles. He encourages pilgrims to define the term for themselves. A miracle, he says, often takes a long time.

In the first century, many Jewish pilgrims to Jerusalem were also seeking miraculous cures. At Bethesda ("house of the double gusher"), northeast of the Temple, there were two springfed pools where the afflicted gathered. When the water bubbled up from below, a few pilgrims at a time were allowed into the pools by the attendants. This turbulence was believed to have a curative power.

On a certain sabbath feast Jesus walked among the handicapped at Bethesda and took particular notice of a man who had endured illness for 38 years. Looking down at the man, inert on his straw mat, Jesus simply asked, "Do you want to be well again?"

What a question! Had the man been mired in self-pity or bitterness, what a diatribe it might have ignited. But the query had to be made so that the man might express his need and his belief that it could be met. "Sir," he said, "I have no one to put me into the pool once the water is disturbed; and when I am still on the way, someone else gets down there before me." Without rancor or whining, he laid his dependence on the line.

For him, there was only Jesus. And for Jesus, at that moment, there was only him—one good person whose bereft being cried out so authentically that it drew the power of healing and health out of the Healer. "Get up," Jesus instructed him, feeling within himself the transfer of power which was already taking place. "Pick up your sleeping mat and walk around!"

Without hesitation, the man arose, unfolding his body and shaking it out like a delightful new wardrobe. Thirty-eight years of expectation, of coming back again and again to the Sheep Pool, of harboring hope for the next time had all converged in this ecstatic victory. The one-time paralytic was bound for glory on his own two feet. Jesus, headed in the same direction, thanked the Father for harvesting joy from this sere stalk of affliction. He embraced the man and received a little jig of gratitude in return.

"Do you want to be well again?" Jesus inquires of us, whatever our maladies of mind or body. "Do you want to be healed?" he inquires, however entrenched our sinful attitudes or stunting habits. Will our "Yes" be as sincere and confident as that of the paralytic? Are we willing to live it as patiently as pilgrims outside the baths at Lourdes? Can we accept the possibility that a miracle may take a long time?

*Jesus, hear us! We want to be healed.*


*Consider:*

Before responding to "Do you want to be well again?" reflect for a few minutes on what physical, mental or spiritual "paralysis" you most want to be liberated from. Recognize that you cannot "Stand up and walk!" without his help.

How will you answer?

*Act:*

Lie down in a solitary place for about 15 minutes. Rest. Be patient. Pray within yourself "Heal me, Lord." Repeat the prayer slowly and gently for a time. Then be silent. Rest in the Healer's presence. Later on, write your response to this experience and any commitment you may want to make to the prayer of a dependent pilgrim.

*Day 22*  *Are you confident I can do this?*
(Mt 9:28)

Scripture context: Mt 9:27-31

---

What I remember best about my confirmation at age 13 is that brisk little slap on the cheek administered with solemnity by the bishop, a looming presence robed in white. I remember too the way he intoned my name with such profundity that it became a goal to be aspired to: "Glo-ri-a An-na Ca-pon-a!"—soldier of Christ, smart young recruit, standing at attention to be fired upon by a battery of doctrinal questions. . . proud as Jeanne d'Arc, resplendent in her white armor, riding into Toulouse. . . ready to take on Satan's legions—or whosoever might be lurking in ambush against a greenhorn confirmandi.

Maybe the theology—or my adolescent understanding of it—was all wrong. But one thing remains. As I stood, garbed in white taffeta and veiled like a nun, I felt thoroughly affirmed. In the auspicious person of the Bishop of Ogdensburg, Brian J. McEntegart, the one, holy, catholic and apostolic church was saying to me, "Gloria Anna, be sealed, confirmed, approved by the gift of the Holy Spirit. We have confidence in you. Go forth! Do great things for the glory of God and the salvation of the world!" I marched to the fanfare of coronets as we strode out of church into the company of our relatives.

There have been times over the years when I've felt taken for granted, ignored or held back by a church that can't quite bring herself to believe her own teachings on equality. Yet, on balance, I've never felt thoroughly unconfirmed, either. The church still has faith that this one-time soldier of Christ can communicate the living Word by the power of the Holy Spirit. (And is not the pen mightier than the sword?) Because she does believe, I am able to do it.

As Jesus was leaving the synagogue area one time, two blind men came tap-tapping after him with their threadbare tunics flapping in the breeze. "Son of David, have mercy on us!" they cried with one voice, like twin cantors. "Have pity on us!" Insulated by a voluble crowd of disciples, the rabbi did not at first hear their entreaties. When he got to the house where he was to dine, however, they caught up with him.

Reaching for him with blind arms and urgent pleas, they again begged for his help. Jesus looked at them, taking in as no one had before the full penalty of their shackles. Then he asked, "Are you confident I can do this?" Do you confirm my ability to heal you? Will your faith rise up to meet mine in this holy act? Are you sure you believe in me?

"Yes, Lord," they told him, no questions raised. The blind men knew and affirmed who Jesus was—Son of David, royal descendant, messiah most probably, miracle-worker most certainly. Yes, Lord, we are as confident of you as we are of the sunrise we have never seen.

At that Jesus touched their eyes and said, "Because of your faith it shall be done to you." Mercy given. Sight received. Gleeful shouts of praise burst from the two who alternately rubbed their eyes and blinked into the face of their liberator. "We knew it! We knew you would do it!" they exclaimed, still in unison, bonded even closer now by a faith so sealed in remarkable recompense.

Because Jesus was not yet ready for what Jerusalem had to offer him, he shushed the new-sighted duo and sternly warned them, "See to it that no one knows of this." He who would calm the angry sea could not, however, muzzle these elated witnesses.

No doubt they agreed to his request, having learned through years of dependency to be artfully diplomatic. (Of course, rabbi. Whatever you say, O wonder-working Jesus of Nazareth, Son of David that you are! Far be it from us to breathe a word of this to anyone.) Yet as soon as they were out of earshot, they raced into the sun-stippled countryside, clamoring his name to every herdsman and beekeeper they could find.

Having endured a half-life for so long, the two men were ready to gallop headlong into the fullness of life Jesus offered them. In generously affirming him, they had freed themselves.

*Son of David, Savior, we confirm you as the one who liberates us to do great things for the glory of God and the salvation of the world.*

90

*Consider:*

"Are you confident I can do this?" How might this inquiry of Jesus relate to a shortcoming or disability that you now feel confined by?

Have you wholeheartedly confirmed Jesus' power to make of you a committed disciple, or a courageous witness for peace and justice? If not, why not?

How will you respond to Jesus in the context of your present spiritual needs?

*Act:*

Name one affirming action you can take to demonstrate your confidence in Jesus as a liberator.

# Day 23     Can you drink the cup that I must drink? *(Mk 10:38)*

*Scripture context: Mk 10:35-40*

---

When Elie Wiesel received the Nobel Peace Prize in 1986, he insisted that it belonged to all the survivors of the Holocaust and their children. They shared in the suffering. They shared the painful memories. They should also share in the glory which Wiesel, as their most notable spokesman, had attracted.

Emerging from Auschwitz at 17, physically and spiritually wasted, Elie Wiesel had to shoulder the knowledge that the rest of his family had perished in the camps. His journey back to faith and purpose took 10 years. But out of that interior suffering came the revelation of his mission. He would be a prophet of remembrance, of forgiveness and of universal brotherhood. Through his writing and lecturing, he would remind Jew and Gentile alike that we are all responsible for one another.

"If we forget," Wiesel insists, referring to the atrocities of the Nazis, "we are guilty, we are accomplices." He speaks for all political prisoners, all victims of brutish torture. To remain silent in the face of any human tragedy is to abdicate our responsibility as a faithful people—whatever our faith.

"Our lives no longer belong to us alone. They belong to all those who need us desperately," the Nobel winner avers.

In accepting the prize, Elie Wiesel stood in silence for three minutes with his head bowed. Then he donned a yarmulke and prayed in Hebrew, then in English, "Blessed be he who has kept us alive to see this day."

Later, explaining his unexpected silence at the podium, Wiesel said that he had seen and drawn strength from his parents and his sister "who had disappeared into the kingdom of the night." He wanted the silence to speak to the crowd about the presence of these other sufferers who equally deserved the world's respect. The prophet's message was heard.

Shortly after Jesus made the first prediction of his passion, James and John came to him with a request that unwittingly revealed their limited understanding of his identity. The strong-minded sons of Zebedee had been mulling over their future.

"Master," they said to Jesus, "We want you to do us a favor." It was a confident approach based on the familial prerogative Jesus had already granted his disciples, "My mother and my brothers are those who hear the word of God and act upon it" (Lk 8:21). James and John knew that the rabbi would give them whatever they asked for—as long as he was convinced it was for their good. The request they had in mind seemed eminently appropriate to them.

Putting an arm around either one, Jesus asked, "What is it you want me to do for you?" They were right. He wanted to indulge them whenever he could because he alone knew how much would be required of them later on. They replied honestly, with no attempt to disguise what might be construed as less than selfless motives. "Allow us to sit, one at your right hand and the other at your left when you come into your glory."

They had envisioned themselves at the head table, and liked what they saw. "What does it matter," they might have speculated, "if we have given up our homes and even our respectability? Someday we will be richly rewarded. People will eye us with envy and say, 'See how wise were Zebedee's sons to devote themselves to the Master's cause. They knew what they were doing after all.'"

Taken aback by their ambitious expectations, Jesus told them bluntly, "You don't know what you are asking. Can you drink the cup that I must drink, or be baptized with the baptism with which I must be baptized?" Did they have any idea how sheer and treacherous was Jesus' path to glory?

Still unabashedly sure of themselves, they answered, "We can." Perhaps they thought of the cold nights spent by the wayside, the empty stomachs imposed at times by their vagabond existence, the scorn of the wealthy and the enmity of the powerful. Perhaps they considered all of the renunciations Jesus would require of them—all except one. "We can," they said. And Jesus took them at their word.

He told them, "The cup that I must drink you shall drink, and with the baptism with which I must be baptized you shall be baptized, but as for seats at my right hand or my left, these are not mine to grant; they belong to those to whom they have been allotted."

The two disciples had pledged their fidelity, agreeing to share with Jesus whatever cup of dark affliction might be offered. And when his suffering was over, they would be his ministers of remembrance, calling the community to share in his dying and in his rising.

Jesus bowed his head. In the silence which was so characteristic of him, he drew strength from those who would go up to Jerusalem with him.

*"Blessed be he who has kept us alive to see this day." May we never knowingly refuse to drink from his cup!*

94

*Consider:*

From which of these cups have you, at different times of your life, been willing to drink with the suffering Christ?

the cup of loneliness (resulting from your fidelity to Gospel values)

the cup of physical deprivation (accepted out of love for Christ or others)

the cup of rejection and misunderstanding

the cup of ingratitude

the cup of serious illness, physical impairment or impending death (your own or that of a loved one)?

How did these experiences affect your solidarity with those who suffer desperately?

Name a cup of suffering which you now fear and/or refuse to accept.

What response will you make to Jesus in regard to this cup?

*Act:*

Call to mind someone (or some group) who is now drinking deeply from one of the cups listed above. What will you do to express your solidarity with him or her?

## Day 24

*Anyone who believes in me, even though that person dies, will live. . . . Do you believe this?* (Jn 11:26)

*Scripture context: Jn 11:1-44*

God knows how many times the phone had rung before I finally woke up. The voice of my friend's husband was weak as if he might be calling from abroad. "Can you come over?" he asked. "Julie just died." That was it. A naked truth demanding acceptance. We had known, of course, that it was coming. Neuroblastoma had no cure. It was a cancer without pity, infecting only young children.

So Julie Ann, aged six, died in her sleep on June 17, 1980, leaving a family of five without daughter and sister.

When I arrived, Albert was still trying to reach our pastor, a priest who had befriended Julie. The professional comfort he was trained to give would relieve us in our amateurs' encounter with death. Doris was kneeling by the couch where her daughter lay, Our Lady of Sorrows contemplating the body of her ravaged Son.

Julie's eyes of painfully beautiful blue were half-open. She looked expectant—as though she had just seen something that pleased her. The wolfish affliction that had stalked her for so long left no tracks. She was radiant, an icon of innocence to be worn ever after like a photograph in a locket.

Doris wept as she told the story of how she had found Julie lifeless in her bed at dawn. "If only she had called out to me," Doris complained, defending herself against misguided guilt. "I could at least have held her in my arms at the end. She died all alone."

I had no words to tranquilize her suffering. The concrete language of a child's dead body shames abstractions into silence. Doris was remembering our pilgrimage to Lourdes and the hopes it had raised when Julie went into remission for several months. But then the cancer had reasserted itself, no longer intimidated by chemotherapy, radiation or rosaries.

"Why couldn't Julie have had a miracle?" Doris demanded. "Why not? Why not?" The same question had been plaguing me, and I wished to heaven the pastor would appear to help us carry the load. "I don't know,

Doris," I said. "I'm so sorry." (Was I apologizing for my own inadequacy or for God's? Was I begging her pardon for not sharing her grief? I felt happy for Julie, happy that the needles and the nausea could never again make her cry. I had already seen her running through a meadow with the Child Jesus to the sound of laughter and sheep's bells.)

Jesus too knew what it was to feel inadequate at a friend's death. Informed of Lazarus' terminal illness, he yet arrived after the fact. Why hadn't he been there to heal, or at least to utter authentic consolation at the last? Seeing her brother's corpse, Martha had wanted to scream at Jesus, to shake him and pound her fists on his faithless chest.

When he finally arrived, four days after the burial, Martha had come to herself. She embraced him and said, "Lord, if you had been here, my brother would not have died." Jesus said nothing, holding her, absorbing some of the pain his absence had caused.

Martha decided to try once again, even now. "I know that God will grant whatever you ask of him." Jesus smiled, receiving her confidence. "Your brother will rise again," he assured her. Thinking she had heard him, Martha affirmed her belief in the general resurrection on the last day.

Jesus held her by the shoulders, opening a space for emphasis between them. "I am the resurrection," he insisted. "Anyone who believes in me, even though that person dies, will live, and whoever lives and believes in me will never die." His hands tightened. "Do you believe this?"

She replied, "Yes, Lord. I believe that you are the Christ, the Son of God, the one who has come into this world." Jesus then sent her off to get her sister who was in the house, insulated by a thick circle of mourners.

Rushing out, Mary threw herself at the rabbi's feet and cried, "Lord, if you had been here my brother would not have died." She chose the very words with which Martha had wounded him. He turned away, hiding his own defenseless sorrow. A profound sigh, as from one who has just been told that his days are numbered, escaped him. He took Mary's hand and, trembling, asked, "Where have you put him?"

The sisters led him to the tomb. Seeing the stone blocking the entrance, Jesus was overcome by its message of human mortality. He turned to see if Martha and Mary were similarly affected. Their faces mirrored faith's costly battle against despair, and Jesus wept.

Among the mourners, some mumbled about why the Master hadn't saved himself—and them—the grief. A man who could make the blind see could assuredly have cured Lazarus. Didn't this dear friend of Jesus deserve a miracle? What good were his tears if that is all he had to offer? The body of Lazarus, rigid on its granite couch, accused him of infidelity.

"Take the stone away," Jesus said. Martha, ever solicitous for her guests, corrected him. Had he forgotten that the stench of death would

98

bowl them all over? Sternly, he responded, "Have I not told you that if you believe you will see the glory of God?" Martha blushed and kept silent.

As the stone was rolled away, Jesus prayed his profound thanks that the Father would now make resurrection a visible reality for those who had doubted it. He commanded, "Lazarus, come out!" Martha clung to Mary in dreadful anticipation. They dared not look at Jesus, but stared at the gaping tomb, willing it to release its prisoner.

Within moments, the linen-wrapped Lazarus emerged, walking like a clown on stilts, his startled face masked in funeral wear. "Unbind him, let him go free," Jesus said triumphantly, as the sisters kissed his hands, anointing him with their tears.

*Jesus, command us to come forth from the dark cave of unbelief!*

*Consider:*

"Anyone who believes in me, even though that person dies, will live. . . . Do you believe this?" Recall the experience of a death in your family or among your friends. Briefly describe your doubts and other feelings about God's "failure" to prevent that person's death.

Compare your experience with Martha's (or with Julie's mother's).

Are you absolutely convinced of resurrection—your own and others'? Explain your response.

*Act:*
To strengthen your faith in resurrection, choose as a prayer partner a friend or relative who has died. For at least one week, pray for and to this person who remains united to you in the communion of saints.

## Day 25    What shall I say, "Father, save me from this hour?" (Jn 12:27)

*Scripture context: Jn 12:20-36*

In a 1987 interview with *Boston Globe* reporter Marian Christy, Martin Sheen described his conversion from Sunday morning Catholic to committed peace activist. At the time of the interview, he had already earned an arrest record for participating in peaceful demonstrations against the nuclear arms race. The respected actor had also donated most of his income from the film "Gandhi" to Mother Teresa, and had worked with Mitch Snyder among the homeless of Washington, D.C.

Admitting that most of his life he had been content to let others take the flak by speaking out for social justice, Sheen said that he could no longer hide from the truth of the gospel. His spiritual director had advised him to apply the teachings of Jesus directly to everyday issues that concerned him. "Love your enemies" and "Blessed are the peacemakers" thus became personal calls to action. Martin Sheen set out to awaken others to the threat of those horrifying weapons which had become "the gods of our idolatry."

The role of a peace activist didn't come naturally. Sheen hated to endanger everything he loved (his family, his success, financial security, power, possessions). Nor did he welcome the degradation of jail. His forthright description of his fears might well unnerve less determined recruits.

"Basically," he told the interviewer, "I'm a coward. When I act on the truth, I tremble. I shake. I throw up. I don't want to face the press. I don't want to risk jail. I don't want to face anything, especially the truth of myself" (*Boston Globe*, March 11, 1987).

Jesus had not been in Jerusalem long when a delegation of Greeks requested of the disciple Philip, "Sir, we should like to see Jesus." Informed of their entreaty, Jesus interpreted this coming of the gentiles as a sign that his hour was soon to come. The holy city beckoned to him like an executioner with unfinished business to attend to.

Preparing his friends for a truth they would rather not know, Jesus spoke of a grain of wheat that had to fall, be buried and trampled on, before it could make itself useful. Then he tightened the focus a little closer by saying, "Anyone who loves his life loses it; anyone who hates his life in this world will keep it for eternal life." The day would come when protecting their own backsides could no longer be a top priority.

Among his listeners, some were thrilled at the prospect of risking their lives for the messiah. The glorious appeal of martyrdom was not lost on them. They were not, however, ready to go on the morrow. Others openly feared the consequences of his words and decided they were not to be taken literally.

Jesus continued in a more inviting tone: "Whoever serves me must follow me and my servant will be with me wherever I am. If anyone serves me, my Father will honor him."

They wanted, with all their zealous hearts, to be where he was whatever the cost. They would serve him as long as they lived. But must a servant also be a sacrifice? And was not a sacrifice always utterly consumed?

They were not alone in their anxieties. Jesus admitted, "How my soul is troubled. What shall I say, 'Father, save me from this hour'?" He shrugged his shoulders and conveyed by his expression that the question was as inappropriate as sackcloth at a wedding feast.

"But it is for this very reason that I have come to this hour," he concluded. So why should he tremble and back off, seeking to be rescued from his own fulfillment? Was he going to be deterred by a few bouts with nausea and the shakes?

"Father, glorify your name!" His sudden prayer was spoken in a loud voice, like that of a lone warrior riding against an armed horde.

*Jesus, stand by us in whatever hour we most dread.*

*Consider:*
Apply this question (What shall I say, "Father, save me from this hour?") to your fear of death, illness, true discipleship, or any other cause that requires you to love your life less and sacrificial service more.

After prayer and reflection (with the help of a spiritual director, if available), what might you do to break through the fear of some specific hour?

*Act:*

To flex your muscles today, speak out, in person or in writing, against some injustice that really matters to you.

# Day 26 *Lay down your life for me?* (Jn 13:38)

*Scripture context: Jn 13:36-38*

---

The 1986 TV drama "Promise" depicted a painful relationship between two brothers, DJ, a nervous and provocative schizophrenic, and Bob, an easy-going self-centered bachelor. At his mother's funeral, Bob, now a middle-aged real estate broker, has to come to terms with the promise he made 30 years earlier, "Mom, I'll always take care of DJ."

He meant it—and still does. But the frustrations of sharing his home with someone who is subject to alternating delusions and catatonic stupors is beginning to make him regret the promise. DJ's mental illness plays havoc with Bob's lifestyle and sets him up for a number of public humiliations. Although he still loves his younger brother and wants to protect him, he resents being robbed of the comfortable existence he had carved out for himself.

In an attempt to reveal his inner torment, DJ tells Bob about the voices in his head, directing him to do things. (That's why he sends for all those veg-o-matics and gut busters advertised on TV. He is convinced the announcers are speaking to him personally.) Then he adds, "In crowds I see people looking at me and talking. Sometimes I hear them planning to kill me. . . ." DJ's terrible need binds Bob to his promise.

At that final feast of Passover, the disciples hardly knew what to make of their enigmatic host. While the others had submitted to the washing of feet with self-conscious asides, Peter had blustered his objections for all to hear. "You shall never wash my feet!" he declared, proud of his manifest humility which refused to play the lord to Jesus' servant.

"If I do not wash you, you can have no share with me," the rabbi had countered. And Peter, whose mother hadn't raised any fools, fell all over himself in complying.

They had no sooner regained their equilibrium than Jesus, visibly troubled, announced that one of them would betray him. His friends were puzzled and put out. Who could he mean? Peter signalled John to coax the answer out of Jesus while the others speculated among themselves. When Judas left quietly, they thought he was off to make a donation to the poor on the occasion of the holy days. Only the beloved disciple understood the betrayer's departure.

"Now has the Son of man been glorified," Jesus began, "and in him God has been glorified." Gathering his friends closer and calling them his children, the rabbi warned that he would soon have to leave them. "Where I am going, you cannot come," he said. (Peter shook his head in denial but held his tongue.) "Love one another," Jesus insisted. Fraternal love would be the emblem of their discipleship.

Peter couldn't stand it any longer. He had to reassure Jesus, no matter how imaginary these betrayal fears turned out to be. The Master's eyes were already brimming. His need for their friendship had never before been so openly displayed.

"Lord," Peter said, sitting close beside him, "where are you going?" Jesus leaned against his sturdy companion and replied, "Now you cannot follow me where I am going, but later you shall follow me."

Feeling the weight of Jesus' sorrow, Peter would have none of it. "Why can I not follow you now? I will lay down my life for you!"

This extravagant promise of brotherly love, erupting from the depths, sounded so right to Peter that he wished he had prefaced it with a little speech, a brief introduction to prepare Jesus for its ultimacy. Now that he had heard himself saying it, Peter was certain he meant it. Who on God's earth was worth dying for if not Jesus the Nazarene? Yes, the disciple told himself. He would most certainly hand over his own life to save his beloved Master. He would be true to his word.

"Lay down your life for me?" Jesus asked. The jagged edges of his voice cut the limb out from under Peter. There was no doubt about the rabbi's meaning. Although the two remained side by side, a cleft had opened between them.

Stung by the question, Peter stroked his beard and stared hard at Jesus, hoping he had somehow misunderstood. That hope was deflated by the prediction Jesus then made. "In all truth, I tell you, before the cock crows you will have disowned me three times."

*Master, may we never betray you in the ones we have promised to love and protect.*

*Consider:*
"Lay down your life for me?" Before responding from the heart as Peter did, reflect on the promises of enduring love you have made during your lifetime.

Which of these promises (if any) have you forgotten, denied or failed to fulfill? Briefly explain why.

Choose one way in which you can promise to lay down your life for Jesus. Share it with him.

*Act:*
Make amends to someone who has been hurt or alienated by your failure to keep a promise.

# Day 27    *Had you not the strength to stay awake one hour? (Mk 14:40)*

*Scripture context: Mk 14:26-42*

---

"One of our main tasks," the Salvadoran woman said, "is resisting anxiety." In that simple understatement, Carmen Elena Hernandez evoked the milieu of sorrow and death in which she and five other members of the Small Community live. The lay women, who minister to the poor in San Salvador, have been followed by military police and threatened with death. One of their number, Silvia Maribel Arriola, has already been killed by the army.

The lay community came together in 1981 after a bomb blast ripped out a wall of the priests' residence at Christ the Savior parish. The priests left. Seven women who had worked in the parish decided to stay. They wanted to "accompany the people" in their daily walk through the hell of poverty and oppression.

Despite their fears, the women have remained in the San Salvador archdiocese, forming basic Christian communities, caring for refugees, visiting prisoners, and mourning with the families of the slain. Their celibate and consecrated lifestyle gives them the strength to endure.

These courageous women of the church find their purpose in the gospel. As Maria Isabel Figuero observes, "We are doing what the gospel demands. And if problems, persecution and even death come to us, then we understand clearly that this is the price that must be paid." (*Maryknoll*, January, 1987, p. 37).

Leaving the upper room, Jesus and his companions made their way in straggling procession to a place called Gethsemane on the Mount of Olives. Inebriated by the evening's revelations and the festal wine, the disciples were not in the mood to contemplate whatever evil waited in ambush. The rabbi's unqualified love for them, indeed for all the daughters and sons of Yahweh, was dizzying. The rest was a bad dream. At dawn they would put their heads together, come up with a plan to evade those who would destroy him.

In the garden, Jesus directed the disciples to an olive grove where they should remain until he returned. Peter, James and John he took with him, moving further into the shadowed recesses of his chosen retreat. No one spoke. Jesus' dark expression had silenced their spirited banter. "He looks like a man whose house has just burned down," Peter thought. "And he doesn't yet know if his wife and children were inside."

Jesus then turned to them and said, "My soul is sorrowful to the point of death." His words fell heavily on them with an unwelcome sobering effect. "Wait here, and stay awake," he insisted, as they instinctively drew nearer to him in his anxiety. Against their better judgment, the disciples settled themselves under a sheltering tree.

Moving further on, out of sight of his friends, Jesus collapsed on the damp night ground. He was a condemned prisoner in solitary confinement. Could the bars of his cell be broken? Was there a trap door he had not yet discovered? Would burly angels come to break him out?

"Abba, Father!" He was a child again, inexplicably locked out of the house, afraid of the dark. But if he could make himself heard, Abba would be there to rescue him. "Abba! For you everything is possible," he prayed, hope rising in his throat. "Take this cup away from me. But let it be as you, not I, would have it."

He pushed himself up to his knees. Cold sweat ran icily down under his arms, down his back, down his legs. Wiping his face with the back of his hand, he got up and returned to the warm circle of his companions. But he found them curled up in their tunics like revelers sleeping off the effects of their feasting. Gripping Peter by the arm, he said, "Simon, are you asleep? Had you not the strength to stay awake one hour?"

At that the others woke up, mumbled their excuses and sat upright, feigning a command of the situation. Jesus reiterated his command, "Stay awake and pray not to be put to the test. The spirit is willing enough but human nature is weak."

His tone says, "Take it from me. I've been there. And it's no picnic. So be on guard!" Ashamed of their short-lived vigilance, Peter, James and John rebuked one another and made a firm decision to keep each other awake.

Jesus again went apart, and repeated his prayer of final obedience, of filial obedience, of fatal obedience. "But let it be as you, not I, would have it." When he returned to find his friends sleeping again, he was more depressed than disillusioned. Human nature is weak. The three wanted nothing more than to keep the vigil with their beloved Lord. Yet they were unable to stand against sleep's inexorable tow.

A third time Jesus prayed, accepting the solitude that so forcibly reminded him of who he was and what he was about to do. ("I lay down my life of my own free will; no one takes it from me.") He returned to his friends and spoke to them with the resignation of a mother who knows her lie-abed sons are going to be late for work again. "You can sleep on now and have your rest. It is all over. The hour has come. Now the Son of man is to be betrayed into the hands of sinners.''

They were about to renew their avowals of faithfulness when Jesus, detecting the arrival of intruders in the garden, said, ''Get up! Let us go! My betrayer is not far away.''

*Jesus, lonely watcher in the night, forgive our weakling vigils for we too are sleep-sogged sentinels.*

*Consider:*

''Had you not the strength to stay awake one hour?'' Reflect on the most telling ''one hour'' Jesus might refer to in your life. Possibilities: being faithful to night prayer when you are exhausted; keeping willing vigil with a sick, depressed or needy friend; staying at the side of one who is dying or facing another traumatic event; remaining alert and responsive to the needs of a trying family member.

What would you say to Jesus about one of those times when he found you wrapped in your tunic and dead to the world?

How do you think Jesus would respond?

*Act:*

Within the next three days, keep a one-hour prayer vigil for whatever intention is closest to your heart. Pray at sunrise or late at night or in the middle of the night (knowing that you are in good monastic company).

# *Day 28*   *Do you ask this of your own accord?*
*(Jn 18:34)*

*Scripture context: Jn 18:33-38*

---

Once, when the police came out in force to arrest him, the priest was bodily protected by his people who knelt, in their thousands, all around the church, so that no one could reach him. And they stayed on their knees until Father Jerzy Popieluszko was safe, temporarily, yet again.

The chaplain of Solidarity, Poland's outlawed labor union, offered his compatriots a new vision of peaceful resistance to government oppression. At his monthly Mass for the Homeland, Father Jerzy intrepidly told the truth about Poland's official atheism and its disastrous toll on the people. He insisted that the church must confront the injustices that were an affront to human dignity. "As he spoke a rare and prayerful silence would descend on the congregation," an observer wrote.

His effectiveness as a prophet and champion of the workers made Jerzy Popieluszko a prime target for the secret police. He was accused of slander and lying, inciting to riot, and, ironically, "abusing freedom of conscience." He was attacked in the press and on the streets. His life was threatened. But he went on.

When the government refused him a passport to Rome, he responded with an eloquent statement of his guiding principle. In part he said, "The source of our captivity lies in the fact that we allow lies to reign, that we do not denounce them, that we do not protest against their existence every day of our lives, that we do not confront lies with the truth but keep silent or pretend to believe in the lies."

To bear witness to the truth, Father Jerzy was willing to risk everything. Shortly before his brutal murder by the police, he gave an English reporter a set of his taped sermons. He told Mary Craig that if he were arrested and false words were put in his mouth by others, he wanted people to hear for themselves what he had said. "I have never done more than speak the truth," he concluded. (*The Tablet*, London, November 10, 1984)

When Jesus, under arrest, was arraigned before Pontius Pilate, the procurator asked, "Are you the king of the Jews?" The prisoner looked back at him, giving no ground. Then he parried with a question of his own.

"Do you ask this of your own accord, or have others said it to you about me?"

That forthright query threw Pilate off his imperial stride. Had he not, in fact, wondered about this strange Galilean who managed to arouse adulation as well as animosity among his own people? Pilate, despite himself, was fascinated by the prisoner's self-possession at a moment when other men would grovel or curse. But he reined in his curiosity, sniffing danger.

To regain the upper hand, Pilate retorted, "Am I a Jew?" He was merely repeating the charge made by the high priests, a charge which he attributed to their political acumen rather than to any wrongdoing on the prisoner's part.

But what a nerve this man had, implying that the procurator might recognize him as some sort of monarch. "What have you done?" Pilate demanded. Jesus was disappointed—not for himself, but for the procurator who had failed to see the truth. However, he was about to give his adversary another opportunity for enlightenment, a chance to speak from a source more authentic than the weekly dispatches from Rome.

"Mine is not a kingdom of this world. If my kingdom were of this world, my men would have fought to prevent my being surrendered to the Jews. As it is, my kingdom does not belong here."

Pilate heard. But he hardened his heart, provoked by the conviction that he was the one under interrogation by the law. This nowhere man, standing bound before him, haggard and God-haunted, calmly claimed to be able to raise up armies. Pilate paced the courtyard. Then he asked abruptly, "So, then you are a king?" (Might he have wanted to make it a declaration rather than a question?)

Jesus knew that the moment for conversion had passed. Pilate would prefer to remain a prisoner, answerable to Caesar and to Caiaphas if not to his own conscience. Years of pretending to believe the lies he lived by bound him as surely as a whipcord. He couldn't afford any trouble over this obscure Jew who might, after all, be as menacing as his accusers claimed.

"It is you who say that I am a king," Jesus responded. "I was born for this, I came into the world for this: to bear witness to the truth; and all who are on the side of truth listen to my voice."

Pulling skepticism over his head like a cowl, Pilate turned away, scoffing, "Truth! What is that?" His were rhetorical questions, stage dialogue to disguise the actor's fears. Habituated to compromise, he could no longer believe in any lasting and impregnable truth on which mortals might rely. Jesus answered him with silence, a silence which confronted Pilate with his own duplicity.

Knowing Jesus to be innocent, Pilate yet allowed the Jews to have their way. Jesus had asked him to speak for himself, to bear witness to the truth.

Now the boat was leaving, pulling off for a distant shore. And Pilate had missed his passage.

*Jesus, make our lives ring true! Amen and amen.*

*Consider:*

"Do you ask this of your own accord?" Is your relationship with Jesus one you have claimed as your own through questioning and doubt, prayer and scripture study, trial and testing? Or does your faith rest more exclusively on what others have told you about him? Briefly explain your response.

In what ways do you bear witness to the truth of the gospel?

*Act:*

What will you do today to avoid "pretending to believe in lies?" (Seek the intercession of Jerzy Popieluszko, martyr and prophet.)

**Day 29**   *Was it not necessary that the Christ should suffer before entering into his glory? (Lk 24:26)*

*Scripture context: Lk 24:13-35*

---

May my tongue cleave to my mouth if I ever again say to someone who has suffered a tragic loss, "It was the will of God." Rather than do without the comfort of an explanation for someone's untimely death, I have obliquely blamed God, fingering him as the culprit as surely as the insurance agent who refers to a tornado causing thousands of deaths, as "an act of God." Whenever I'm tempted to rely on facile words in the wake of sorrow, I'll remember William Sloane Coffin, Jr.

The long-time Yale chaplain and liberal activist lost his 24-year-old son a few years ago. Alex died when his car went off a rain-slicked road into Boston Harbor. A well-intentioned woman commented to Coffin, "I just don't understand the will of God."

Enraged, the bereaved father angrily enumerated for her the many ways in which Alex could have avoided the accident. Unnatural deaths, Coffin insisted, are never God's will. When his son's car disappeared beneath the black waves that night, "God's heart was the first of all hearts to break," he said.

His comment reminded me of a telling insight from the poet Rainer Maria Rilke. Speculating on the essence of life, he considers who, among all created beings, actually lives life. The poem concludes:

> Is it the warm beasts, moving to and fro,
> Is it the birds strange as they sail from view?
> This life—who lives it really? God, do you?
> ("Although as from a prison walled with hate," *Book of Hours*, p. 39)

We may not know why we suffer so much, why so many children die of hunger, why innocent people are victimized, why our sons and daughters wind up in a shallow grave in North Vietnam or a deep one in Boston Harbor. But we do know who suffers with us, who suffered for us, and whose heart is the first to break.

Was not the Father's heart rent by the harrowing cry of his only Son from the cross, "My God, my God, why have you forsaken me?" (Why have you crossed me off your list, kicked me out of your house, left me in the lurch, deserted me in my hour of need?) Perhaps it was more devastating yet when the faithful Son, with his last breath, gave himself to the Father who had not come to save him. "Father, into your hands I commend my spirit."

The disciples, in hiding, were haunted by his death. He was gone. They had done nothing to rescue him from his enemies. Neither had Yahweh—which, for these men and women of faith, was a paralyzing reality. Why was God himself among the missing persons when Jesus needed him most? Why had the Messiah been allowed to die like some disreputable criminal? Why, God? Why now, God? Why?

On the third day, Mary of Magdala, Joanna and Mary had come to the Twelve with astounding news. The tomb was empty. "He is not here; he has risen!" The women kept repeating the seven laconic words of the angelic messengers. They rejoiced and rushed to tell whoever would listen to them. But Peter and the others were still uncertain. If Jesus were risen, where was he now? Was he too in hiding?

On that same day, two of those who had followed Jesus were on their way to Emmaus. While they were lost in conversation about the import of the angels' message, a stranger joined them. "What are all these things that you are discussing as you walk along?" he inquired, falling into step with them.

Cleopas looked at him as though he had his tunic on inside out. "You must be the only person staying in Jerusalem who does not know the things that have been happening there these last few days," he commented, with a touch of condescension. Obligingly, the stranger took up his cue, saying, "What things?"

The disciples recited, with proprietary pride, the story of the prophet Jesus of Nazareth who had come to a tragic end at the hands of the chief priests and their Roman colluders. "Our own hope had been that he would be the one to set Israel free," one of them said, in the resigned tones of a religious person who doesn't quite believe his prayer will be answered. They were left with an empty tomb. So what were they to think?

The traveler stopped, regarding them incredulously in his turn. "You foolish men!" he exclaimed, "So slow to believe all that the prophets have said!" Cleopas and his friend might have been insulted had they not been so taken with the stranger's obvious zeal.

"Was it not necessary that the Christ should suffer before entering into his glory?" he asked. (Use your head for something besides a yarmulke rack, brothers. Where were you when Isaiah and Jeremiah were passing out the messianic prophecies?)

His impassioned commentary kept them absorbed all the way to Emmaus. He might have gone on all night, mesmerizing them with the sacred music of his theme. However, one of the disciples had noticed a lodging house where they might spend the night. So the two hearers of the word urged the rabbi to remain with them.

He joined them at the table, assuming the host's role as naturally as he had made himself their teacher. Taking the bread in his hands as though he were cupping the face of his beloved, he pronounced a blessing over it, broke it twice and distributed it to them while looking into the eyes of each.

In that divine gesture, so perfectly his, they recognized Jesus and were about to embrace him when he vanished from their sight.

They hugged one another instead and laughed like children let out of school. "Did not our hearts burn within us," Cleopas began, and without missing a beat his companion continued, "as he talked to us on the road and explained the scriptures to us?"

That set them to laughing again, and they slapped one another on the back, toasted the Messiah, wrapped in a towel the remaining bread which his hands had held, and set out for Jerusalem by the way they had come.

*Messiah, may we recognize in you the thorn-strewn road to glory.*

*Consider:*

"Was it not necessary that the Christ should suffer before entering into his glory?" Interpreting this as a question about your acceptance and experience of suffering, briefly describe how your relationship with Jesus has been changed by whatever you know of the cross.

Share with Jesus your inability to recognize his presence with you in some past or present suffering. Ask him to teach you as he taught the two on the road to Emmaus.

*Act:*

Read a poem, listen to music, or contemplate a work of art that helps you to believe in the redemptive and transforming power of suffering in Jesus' name.

# Day 30 *Do you love me?* *(Jn 21:16)*

*Scripture context: Jn 21:15-19*

---

"I beg your pardon," sang Loretta Lynn, with pardonable pragma-
tism, "I never promised you a rose garden." Not meaning to be disrespect-
ful, I can't help wondering if Andrew and his companion (with whom we
started this journey) would have been so eager to hang around where Jesus
lived had they realized just how many briar patches they would have to pass
through. All those nights on the road, the heckling of the skeptics, the
harassment by the Sanhedrin, the hunger and the doing without, the loss
of friends who were sure the disciples were being led down the path of de-
lusion, the anxiety of accepting a messiah who could be tromped on by Jew
and Roman alike, the inevitable necessity of having to lay down one's life
for one's friends. Jesus never promised his friends an earthly rose garden.

In the beginning, however, it often feels like Eden. We walk the road
with him and little more is required of us than to enjoy the good company.
But sooner or later we notice the pebble in our shoe. The shadow of Jerusalem lengthens. Some of our fellow pilgrims catch his drift and decide to
turn back. When the landscape goes Saharan on us, we catch the Master by
the sleeve of his tunic and try to reason with him. "Heaven preserve us,
Lord, this must not happen to me" (see Mt 16:22).

By the time the disciples share that unexpected post-resurrection
breakfast on the shore, Peter has endured his share of insomnia and self-
recrimination. His threefold denial of Christ still generates waking night-
mares in which the appointed shepherd cravenly flees at the first wolf's
howl.

Whenever he finds himself in dialogue with the Risen Jesus, Peter
gazes earthward as though his sandals might need adjusting. Even when he
struggles ashore, ungainly as a beached cod in his drenched clothing, the
disciple manages to embrace the Master without ever looking into his be-
mused face.

As soon as the others arrive, Peter rushes onto the boat, rather than
risk more moments alone with Jesus, and insists on dragging off the net
with its 153-fish cargo. The Master, his appearance altered yet appealingly
the same, bends over the charcoal fire and hums quietly while he works.

Peter hustles about, taking refuge in usefulness. "Come and eat your meal," says the host, inviting them all, but focusing on the one with the deepest circles under his eyes.

Peter's confidence is restored by the meal. While the others wash down the boat and clean the rest of the catch, he joins Jesus in gazing out to sea. The two sit back on their heels, at ease in their silence, for several minutes.

Then Jesus, his eyes riveted on the water, asks in a voice as still as the Galilee becalmed, "Simon, son of John, do you love me more than these?"

The disciple's heart lurches as though someone had come up behind him and thrown him bodily into the sea. Oh, Adonai, save me, lest I drown in my own unworthiness! Aloud, he answers, "Yes, Lord, you know that I love you." Please believe me. Please make me believable. Moments pass. Peter holds his breath. "Feed my lambs," Jesus says.

Relief rolls over the disciple, then lifts him up on a gathering wave. He knows he has been confirmed. His past sin, having done its work, has been put behind the Lord's back. All is well between them. Better than ever. Ah, the sweet, ennobling joy of being reconciled!

Unaccountably, Jesus repeats his question in a more emphatic manner. "Simon, son of John, do you love me?" Oh-oh! Is this a test? Or does he just need reassurance? Remembering the vulnerable Master who had once asked, "Do you want to leave me, too?" Peter gladly responds, "Yes, Lord, you know that I love you." Jesus pauses again, turning only slightly toward his companion. "Tend my sheep," he says.

Waiting now for Jesus to move on to specifics (How shall I feed? How tend?), Peter is genuinely shocked when the Rabbi turns full face and asks in a pointed tone, "Simon, son of John, do you love me?"

Hurt to the core, the disciple reddens under his beard. But he does not avert his eyes. With the fire-tried conviction of a bridegroom speaking his vows, he answers, "Lord, you know everything. You know well that I love you."

Satisfied, Jesus says, "Feed my sheep."

They sit together, listening to the water coyly slapping the boat, the disciples jesting at their labors. Peter lapses into daydreaming about the heroic deeds he will perform to prove himself a reliable guardian of the flock. That is just the point Jesus speaks to, but in a direction Peter has not envisioned.

"In all truth I tell you, when you were young you put on your belt and walked where you liked." Peter readily smiles, recalling love's early stages. "But," Jesus goes on, "when you grow old you will stretch out your hands, and somebody else will put a belt around you and take you where you would rather not go."

For a second only, an image of crucifixion sears Peter's brain. But it passes like a specter in the night. The sun is still warm. The sea still kind. Jesus is standing now, holding out his hand.

"Follow me," he says.

*Jesus, Lord and Constant Lover, call us in your wake.*

*Consider:*

"Do you love me?" This was no idle question for Peter. Nor is it for us. Among its implications: Do you love me more than those who have not irrevocably accepted me as the driving force of their lives? Do you love me enough to face persecution and imprisonment and even death because your love gives you no alternative? Do you love me enough to walk in a direction you have not chosen to go?

What will your considered response be?

*Act:*

Be a shepherd today in a way that costs you a "little death." (Ideas: Give the money for some purchase you really want to the poor. Give the time you need for an important task or a desired pleasure to some group that is working for peace or justice.)

# Retreat Decisions

---

(After completing Day 30, allow a few days to pass before considering how you hope to integrate the retreat experience.)

## *Part One: Seeking Guidance*

1. What do you want? (Jn 1:38)
2. What do you want from me? (Jn 2:4)
3. You know me and you know where I come from? (Jn 7:28)
4. Do you believe in the Son of Man? (Jn 9:35)
5. Why do you not understand what I say? (Jn 8:43)
6. Why are you so frightened? (Mk 4:40)
7. Why did you doubt? (Mk 14:31)
8. Why do you ask me about what is good? (Mt 19:17)
9. Why not judge for yourselves what is upright? (Lk 12:57)
10. What can we say that the kingdom is like? (Mk 4:30)

Review your responses to the journal questions for Days 1-10. Record here the question of Jesus in Part One that helped you more than any other to know yourself.

Decide how you will continue to be guided by this question in your daily life.

Which of the first 10 questions of Jesus called you most insistently to some kind of conversion?

How do you hope to respond to this call in prayer and action?

Are there other insights about who God is or who you are that you want to retain from Part One? If so, record them here.

## Part Two: Seeking Growth

11. Now, will God not see justice done? (Lk 18:7)
12. Why does this generation demand a sign? (Mk 8:12)
13. Are you not worth much more than they are? (Mt 6:27)
14. For if you love those who love you, what reward will you get? (Mt 5:46)
15. If you lend to those from whom you hope to get money back, what credit can you expect? (Lk 6:34)
16. Why do you observe the splinter in your brother's eye? (Lk 6:41)
17. Which of these three, do you think, proved himself a neighbor? (Lk 10:36)
18. Must he be grateful to the servant? (Lk 17:9)

19. For who is the greater, the one at table or the one who serves? (Lk 22:27)

20. Do you suppose I am here to bring peace on earth? (Lk 12:51)

Review your responses to the journal questions for Days 11-20. Record here the question of Jesus that presented the greatest challenge to you.

How do you hope to continue taking up that challenge in your daily life?

Which of the Part Two questions of Jesus did you experience as most affirming?

How might you strengthen this aspect or your spirituality, or help others to do so?

Other insights from Part Two which you want to retain?

## *Part Three: Seeking Glory*

21. Do you want to be well again? (Jn 5:6)
22. Are you confident I can do this? (Mt 9:28)
23. Can you drink the cup that I must drink? (Mk 10:38)
24. Anyone who believes in me, even though that person dies, will live. . . . Do you believe this? (Jn 11:26)
25. What shall I say, ''Father, save me from this hour''? (Jn 12:27)
26. Lay down your life for me? (Jn 13:38)
27. Had you not the strength to stay awake one hour? (Mk 14:40)
28. Do you ask this of your own accord? (Jn 21:16)
29. Was it not necessary that the Christ should suffer before entering into his glory? (Lk 24:26)
30. Do you love me? (Jn 21:16)

Review your responses to the journal questions for Days 21-30.

Record here the question of Jesus in Part Three which you least want to confront right now.

What does your resistance to this question tell you about yourself?

How could you prepare the way for this question in your life?

Which of the questions in Part Three did you take most to heart?

How might you allow this question to lead you further along the path to glory?

Other insights from Part Three which you want to retain?

# Closing Prayer

Jesus, just and loving
Inquisitor of hearts,
I have encountered you
in gospel arena
braced myself
like a fighter
to receive your truth.
Be my guide,
goad to growth,
path to glory.
Make me bold and artful
in trading talents
entrusted to me,
returning them
fivefold.
(For if I bury them
in old habits,
darkness claims me
once again.)
Rabbi! Make me
a valiant servant
of your truth.
Let me know myself,
know you.
Amen.

# DATE DUE

| | | | |
|---|---|---|---|
| | | | |
| | | | |
| | | | |
| | | | |
| | | | |
| | | | |
| | | | |
| | | | |
| | | | |
| | | | |
| | | | |
| | | | |
| | | | |
| | | | |
| | | | |
| | | | |

HIGHSMITH   #LO-45220